DATE

The Man Made of Words

THE MAN

Essays,

MADE

Stories,

OF

Passages

WORDS

N. Scott Momaday

St Martin's Griffin New York

For Yvor Winters and Janet Lewis

Title page: *Self Portrait* by N. Scott Momaday, courtesy
of Cline LewAllen Contemporary

Production Editor: David Stanford Burr
Design: Songhee Kim

Library of Congress Cataloging-in-Publication Data

Momaday, N. Scott.
    The man made of words : essays, stories, pas-
sages / N. Scott Momaday.—1st ed.
       p. cm.
  ISBN 0-312-15581-6
    1. Indians of North America—Literary collec-
tions. 2. Indians of North America—Civilization.
I. Title.
PS3563.047M66   1997
813'.54—dc21   96-46492
                                         CIP

First Edition: May 1997

10 9 8 7 6 5 4 3 2

Contents

part three:
THE STORYTELLER AND HIS ART

Preface

The essays, stories, and passages in this volume are in some ways the reflections of one who has wandered far and wide in the world, has seen many things, and has recorded the experiences which most excited the days and nights of his journey. They may seem random observations, recollections, and evocations of place and procession. Such an impression does not offend me. My aesthetic sensibilities are such that they can accommodate pronounced variation and spontaneity. Besides, I do not think that these works are random at all. Rather I perceive the writings herein as the pieces of a whole, each one the element of an intricate but unified design. They are the facets of a verbal prism, if you will, patterns like the constellations. The design, in this instance, is the very information of language, that miracle of symbols and sounds that enable us to think, and therefore to define ourselves as human beings.

These pieces were written over a considerable span of time, something over thirty years. And they were of course written by different writers. The man who wrote "The Morality of Indian Hating," a graduate student in the sixties, was certainly not the man who wrote "A Divine Blindness" decades later, although they were set down with the same hand. I trust that the collection reflects something of growth and maturation, that wonderful progression from birth to death that all of us hope to register truly in our minds and hearts. And we are especially blessed who can and must register that odyssey in words.

As long as I can remember, I have been enchanted by words. When I was a very young child I learned the meanings of Kiowa as well as English words, for although my parents spoke to me in English (they and I were a camp within a camp), Kiowa was the language of the homestead on Rainy Mountain Creek in Oklahoma, where I heard my first words. I learned for example the Kiowa word *bae-sau,* which means "sit," or "be seated." I took possession of the word and its meaning almost at once. But the English word *sit* has more meanings than does the Kiowa word, and some of those meanings admit of abstractions that are difficult for a child. How do we confront a word with an array of meanings and consequent meanings? The complexity of language is the quality that gives words their great vitality. We cannot exhaust the power of words; that power is intrinsic. When I say "sit" to my dog, he sits more often than not. But when I say "sit in judgment," I have entered into the complexity of my own mind, and I have isolated myself irrevocably from the command to my dog. I have committed myself, consciously or unconsciously, to my humanity.

We exist in the element of language. Someone has said that to think is to talk to oneself. The implications of this equation are crucial. Language is necessary to thought, and thought (as it is manifested in language) distinguishes us humans from all other creatures.

In the equation above, we might substitute the word *imagination* for "thought." For surely imagination proceeds from language in the very way that thought does, to the extent that we can separate thought and imagination.

Language is the stuff of the imagination. The imagination is the creative aspect of language. It enables us to use language to its highest potential. It enables us to realize a reality beyond the ordinary, it enables us to create and to re-create ourselves in story and literature. It is the possible accomplishment of immortality.

Stories are composed of words and of such implications as the storyteller places upon the words. The choice of words, their arrangement, and their effect are by and large determined by the storyteller. The storyteller exercises nearly complete control over the storytelling experience.

There are different kinds of stories. The basic story is one that centers upon an event. With the exception of epic matter and certain creation myths, stories in the American Indian oral tradition are short. Concentration is a principal quality of their structure. Stories are formed. The form of the story is particular and perceptible.

Stories are true to our common experience; they are statements which concern the human condition. To the extent that the human condition involves moral considerations, stories have moral implications. Beyond that, stories are true in that they are established squarely upon belief. In the oral tradition stories are told not merely to entertain or to instruct; they are told to be believed. Stories are not subject to the imposition of such questions as true or false, fact or fiction. Stories are realities lived and believed. They are true.

The storyteller is the one who tells the story. To say this is to say that the storyteller is preeminently entitled to tell the story. He is original and creative. He creates the storytelling experience and himself and his audience in the process. He exists in the person of the storyteller for the sake of telling the story. When he is otherwise occupied, he is someone other than the storyteller. His telling of the story is a unique performance. The storyteller creates himself in the sense that the mask he wears for the sake of telling the story is of his own making, and it is never the same. He creates his listener in the sense that he determines the listener's existence within, and in relation to, the story, and it is never the same. The storyteller says in effect: "On this occasion I am, for I imagine that I am; and on this occasion you are, for I imagine that you are. And this imagining is the burden of the story, and indeed it is the story."

part one

THE MAN
MADE OF WORDS

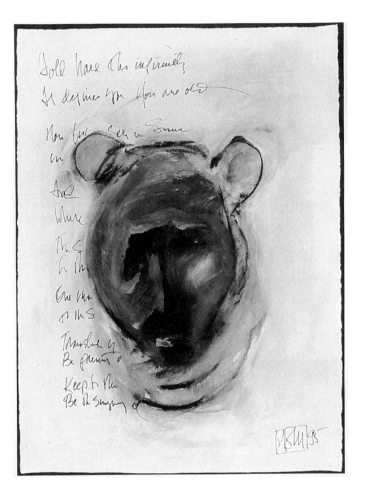

Introduction

A landscape that is incomparable, a time that is gone forever, and the human spirit, which endures.

—The Way to Rainy Mountain

Language fascinates me. I am not a linguist, nor have I real possession of any language but English. From the time I was born my parents spoke to me in English, for that was my mother's native tongue, and she could speak no other. My father, however, was a Kiowa, and English was his second language. Kiowa was the language of the first home in which I lived. The house and the arbor of the homestead on Rainy Mountain Creek in Oklahoma crackled and rang with Kiowa words, exclamations, and songs that even now I keep in my ear. But I would learn only a part of the whole, and I would never learn to converse easily in Kiowa. Those who spoke directly and most often to me were my parents. My Kiowa family spoke to me in broken English, or their Kiowa words were translated into English for me by my father. Now when I hear Kiowa spoken—mostly by the older people who are passing away—it is to me very good. The meaning most often escapes me, but the sound is like a warm wind that arises from my childhood. It is the music of memory. I have come to know that much of the power and magic and beauty of words consist not in meaning but in sound. Story-tellers, actors, and children know this, too. The linguists have had a hard time classifying the Kiowa language. I remember when it was thought to be Caddoan, then Uto-Aztecan. Now I am told that it is Tanoan. It is a mysterious language, and the mystery of it excites my mind. The Kiowas came from the north, but their language is not like the northern languages.

The Kiowas migrated from the Yellowstone to the southern plains, arriving at the Washita River drainage in the early 1700s. They were hunters and nomads and storytellers, and on the southern plains they lived a golden age. They defined the warrior ideal, and they brought the so-called horse culture or centaur culture to its fullest expression.

My father told me stories from the Kiowa oral tradition even before I could talk. Those stories became permanent in my mind, the nourishment of my imagination for the whole of my life. They are among the most valuable gifts that I have ever been given.

The Arrowmaker

The story of the arrowmaker, the "man made of words," is perhaps the first story I was told. My father loved to tell it to me, and I loved to hear it. It remains for me one of the most intensely vital stories in my experience, not only because it is a supernal example of the warrior idea—an adventure story in the best sense—but because it is a story about story, about the efficacy of language and the power of words. One does not come to the end of such a story. I have lived with the story of the arrowmaker for many years, and I am sure that I do not yet understand it in all of its consequent meanings. Nor do I expect to understand it so. The stories I keep close to me, day by day, are those that yield more and more of their spirit in time.

If an arrow is well made, it will have tooth marks upon it. That is how you know. The Kiowas made fine arrows and straightened them in their teeth. Then they drew them to the bow to see that they were straight.

Once there was a man and his wife. They were alone at night in their tepee. By the light of a fire the man was making arrows. After a while he caught sight of something. There was a small opening in the tepee where two hides had been sewn together. Someone was there on the outside, looking in. The man went on with his work, but he said to his wife, "Someone is standing outside. Do not be afraid. Let us talk easily, as of ordinary things." He took up an arrow and straightened it in his teeth; then, as it was right for him to do, he drew it to the bow and took aim, first in this direction and then in that. And all the while he was talking, as if to his wife. But this is how he spoke: "I know that you are there on the outside, for I can feel your eyes upon me. If you are a Kiowa, you will understand what I am saying, and you will speak your name." But there was no answer, and the man went on in the same way, pointing the arrow all around. At last his aim fell upon the place where his enemy stood, and he let go of the string. The arrow went straight to the enemy's heart.

Until very recently the story of the arrowmaker has been the private possession of a few, a tenuous link in that most ancient chain of language which we call the oral tradition; tenuous because the tradition itself appears to be so, for as many times as the story has been told, it has always been but one generation removed from extinction. That is to say, it has been neither more nor less durable than the human voice, and neither more nor less concerned to express the meaning of the human condition.

The story of the arrowmaker is a remarkable act of the imagination, a realization of words and meanings that is altogether simple and direct, yet nonetheless rare and profound, and it illustrates more clearly than anything else in my own experience something of the essential character of the imagination—and in particular of that personification which in this instance emerges from it: the man made of words.

It is important that the story of the arrowmaker returns in a special way upon itself. It is about language, after all, and it is therefore part and parcel of its own subject. Virtually, there is no difference between the telling and that which is told. The point of the story lies not so much in what the arrowmaker does, but in what he says—and, indeed, *that* he says it. The principal fact is that he speaks, and in so doing he places his very life in the balance.

It is this aspect of the story which interests me most, for it is here that the language becomes most conscious of itself; here we are very close to the origin and object of literature; here our sense of the verbal dimension is very keen, and we are aware of something in the nature of language that is at once perilous and compelling. "If you are a Kiowa, you will understand what I am saying, and you will speak your name." Everything is ventured in this simple declaration, which is also a question and a plea.

Precisely at this moment is the arrowmaker realized completely, and his reality consists in language. Implicit in his simple speech is all of his definition and all of his destiny, and by implication all of ours. He ventures to speak because he must; language is the repository of his whole knowledge, and it represents the only chance he has for survival. Instinctively and with great care he deals in the most honest and basic way with words. "Let us talk easily, as of ordinary things," he says. And of the ominous unknown he asks only the utterance of a name, only the most nominal sign that he is understood, that a word or a syllable is returned to him on the sheer edge of meaning. But there is no answer, and the arrowmaker knows at once what he has not known before: that his enemy is, and is present, and that he, the arrowmaker, has gained a crucial advantage over him. Make no mistake, the words of the arrowmaker reveal his peril clearly. The presence outside is decidedly an enemy; twice the storyteller tells us so. The venture is complete and irrevocable, and it ends in the restoration of order and well-being.

The story is meaningful. It is so because it is in the nature of language that it proceeds to the formulation of meaning. Moreover, the story of the arrowmaker especially centers upon this procession of words toward meaning. It seems in fact to turn upon the very idea that language involves the elements of risk and responsibility; and in this it seeks to confirm itself. In a word, it seems to say, everything is a risk. That may well be true, and it may also be that the whole of literature rests upon that truth.

The story of the arrowmaker is supremely metaphorical; indeed it is acutely and incisively a story about story; it is both an example and a definition of literature. It is complex, and yet it is clear; it seems to give more and more of itself in time. Clear it is, and yet there is a kind of resistance in it, as in a riddle; it is the richer for that. It is a kind of prism.

The arrowmaker is preeminently the man made of words. He has consummate being in language; it is the world of his origin and of his posterity, and there is no other. But it is a world of definite reality and of infinite possibility. I have come to believe that there is a sense in which the arrowmaker has a quality of being that is more viable than that of men in general—he has nearly a perfect right to be. We can imagine him, and he imagines himself, whole and vital, going on into the unknown darkness and beyond.

And yet the story has it that he is cautious and alone, and we are given to understand that his peril is great and immediate, and that he confronts it in the only way he can. I have no doubt that this is true. Language determines the arrowmaker, and his story determines our literary experience.

A word, then, on an essential irony which marks the story and gives peculiar substance to the man made of words. The storyteller is nameless and unlettered. We know very little about him, except that in the story is his presence and his mask. And that is enough. He tells of his life in language, and of the risk involved. It occurs to us that he is one with the arrowmaker, and that he has survived, by word of mouth, beyond other men. For the storyteller, for the arrowmaker, language does indeed represent the only chance for survival. It is appropriate that he survives in our time and that he has survived over a period of untold generations.

The Native Voice in American Literature

I

Write: *to draw or form by or as by scoring or incising a surface*
—WEBSTER'S SEVENTH NEW COLLEGIATE DICTIONARY

Imagine: somewhere in the prehistoric distance a man holds up in his hand a crude instrument—a brand, perhaps, or something like a daub or a broom bearing pigment—and fixes the wonderful image in his mind's eye to a wall or rock. In that instant is accomplished really and symbolically the advent of art. That man, apart from his remarkable creation, is all but impossible to recall, and yet he is there in our human parentage, deep in our racial memory. In our modern, sophisticated terms, he is primitive and preliterate, and in the long reach of time he is utterly without distinction, except: he draws. And his contribution to posterity is inestimable; he makes a profound difference in our lives, who succeed him by millennia. For all the stories of all the world proceed from the moment in which he makes his mark. All literatures issue from his hand.

Language and literature involve sacred matter. Among sacred places in America, places of ancient origin and deepest mystery, there is one that comes to my mind again and again. At Barrier Canyon, Utah, there are some twenty sites at which are preserved prehistoric rock art. One of these, known as the Great Gallery, is particularly arresting. Among arched alcoves and long ledges of rock is a wide sandstone wall on which are drawn large, tapering anthropomorphic forms, colored in dark red pigment. There on the geologic picture plane is a procession of gods approaching inexorably from the earth. They are informed with irresistible power; they are beyond our understanding, masks of infinite possibility. We do not know what they mean, but we know that we are involved in their meaning. They persist through time in the imagination, and we cannot doubt that they are invested with the very essence of language, the language of story and myth and primal song. They are two thousand years old, more or less, and they remark as closely as anything can the origin of American literature.

The native voice in American literature is indispensable. There is no true literary history of the United States without it, and yet it has not been clearly delineated in our scholarship. The reasons for this neglect are perhaps not far to find. The subject is formidable; the body of songs, prayers, spells, charms, omens, riddles, and stories in Native American oral tradition, though constantly and considerably diminished from the time of European contact, is large, so large as to discourage investigation. The tradition has evolved over a very long and unrecorded period of time in numerous remote and complex languages, and it reflects a social and cultural diversity that is redoubtable. Research facilities are inadequate by and large, and experts in the field are few. Notwithstanding, the need is real and apparent.

Ancestors of modern American Indians were at the top of North America as early as 25,000 years ago. They were hunters whose survival was predicated upon the principle of mobility. Their dispersal upon the continent was rapid. In the hard environment of the far north there remains little evidence of their occupation, but they knew how to make fire and tools, and they lived as we do in the element of language.

American literature begins with the first human perception of the American landscape expressed and preserved in language. *Literature* we take commonly to comprehend more than writing. If writing means visible constructions within a framework of alphabets, it is not more than six or seven thousand years old, we are told. Language, and in it the formation of that cultural record which is literature, is immeasurably older. Oral tradition is the foundation of literature.

II

If verbal artistry is the essence of literature, then it need not be preserved in writing to be worthy of the name.
                    —JOHN BIERHORST, *IN THE TRAIL OF THE WIND.*

A comparison of the written and oral traditions is of course a matter of the greatest complexity. Those who make this comparison are irrevocably committed to the written tradition. Writing defines the very terms of our existence. We cannot know what it is to exist within an oral tradition, or we cannot know entirely. But we can know more than we do, and it behooves us to learn as much as we can, if for no other reason than to gain possession of invaluable resources that are rightfully ours, to discover, that is, a great and legitimate part of our literary heritage.

Writing engenders in us certain attitudes toward language. It encourages us to take words for granted. Writing has enabled us to store vast quantities of words indefinitely. This is advantageous on the one hand but dangerous on the other. The result is that we have developed a kind of false security where language is concerned, and our sensitivity to language has deteriorated. And we have become in proportion insensitive to silence.

But in the oral tradition one stands in a different relation to language. Words are rare and therefore dear. They are jealously preserved in the ear and in the mind. Words are spoken with great care, and they are heard. They matter, and they must not be taken for granted; they must be taken seriously and they must be remembered.

With respect to the oral tradition of the American Indian, these attitudes are reflected in the character of the songs and stories themselves. Perhaps the most distinctive and important aspect of that tradition is the way in which it reveals the singer's and the storyteller's respect for and belief in language.

At the heart of the American Indian oral tradition is a deep and unconditional belief in the efficacy of language. Words are intrinsically powerful. They are magical. By means of words can one bring about physical change in the universe. By means of words can one quiet the raging weather, bring forth the harvest, ward off evil, rid the body of sickness and pain, subdue an enemy, capture the heart of a lover, live in the proper way, and venture beyond death. Indeed, there is nothing more powerful. When one ventures to speak, when he utters a prayer or tells a story, he is dealing with forces that are supernatural and irresistible. He assumes great risks and responsibilities. He is clear and deliberate in his mind and in his speech; he will be taken at his word. Even so, he knows that he stands the chance of speaking indirectly or inappropriately, or of being mistaken by his hearers, or of not being heard at all. To be careless in the presence of words, on the inside of language, is to violate a fundamental morality.

But one does not necessarily speak in order to be heard. It is sometimes enough that one places one's voice on the silence, for that in itself is a whole and appropriate expression of the spirit. In the native American oral tradition, expression, rather than communication, is often first in importance. Singing of the Yeibichai, for example, the mountain spirits of the Navajos, the singers chant in the spirits' strange and urgent language, a language that is unintelligible to us mortals. Although meaningless in the ordinary sense of the word, the chant is nonetheless deeply moving and powerful beyond question.

In this sense, silence too is powerful. It is the dimension in which ordinary and extraordinary events take their proper places. In the Indian world, a word is spoken or a song is sung not against, but within the silence. In the telling of a story, there are silences in which words are anticipated or held on to, heard to echo in the still depths of the imagination. In the oral tradition, silence is the sanctuary of sound. Words are wholly alive in the hold of silence; there they are sacred.

Properly speaking, then, language is sacred. It will not suffice to say that the verbal and the sacred are related; they are indivisible. Consider this ritual formula from the Navajo:

> *Reared within the Mountains!*
> *Lord of the Mountains!*
> *Young Man!*

Chieftain!
I have made your sacrifice.
I have prepared a smoke for you.
My feet thou restore for me.
My legs thou restore for me.
My body thou restore for me.
My mind thou restore for me.
My voice thou restore for me.
Restore all for me in beauty.
Make beautiful all that is before me.
Make beautiful all that is behind me.
It is done in beauty.
It is done in beauty.
It is done in beauty.
It is done in beauty.

This has the formality of prayer and the measure of poetry. It is immediately and essentially religious in its tone and statement. That is to say, the attitude that informs it is holy. In such a formulaic context as this, where the words are precisely fitted into the context of religious ceremony, the oral tradition achieves a remarkable stability, an authority not unlike that of Scripture.

It is significant that in this rich, ceremonial song the singer should end upon the notion of beauty, of beauty in the physical world, of man in the immediate presence and full awareness of that beauty. And it is significant, indeed necessary, that this whole and aesthetic and spiritual sense should be expressed in language. Man has always tried to represent and even to re-create the world in words. The singer affirms that he has a whole and irrevocable investment in the world. His words are profoundly simple and direct. He acknowledges the sacred reality of his being in the world, and to that reality he makes his prayer as an offering, a pledge of his integral involvement, commitment, and belief. He aspires to the restoration of his body, mind, and soul, an aim which in his cultural and religious frame of reference is preeminently an aesthetic consideration, a perception of well-ordered being and beauty, a design of which he is the human center. And the efficacy of his prayer is realized even as he makes it; it is done in beauty.

Often the words are returned upon themselves in a notable and meaningful way. They transcend their merely symbolic value and become one with the idea they express. They are not then intermediate but primary; they are at once the names of things and the things named.

> *You have no right to trouble me,*
> *Depart, I am becoming stronger;*
> *You are now departing from me,*
> *You who would devour me;*
> *I am becoming stronger, stronger.*
> *Mighty medicine is now within me,*
> *You cannot now subdue me—*
> *I am becoming stronger,*
> *I am stronger, stronger, stronger.*

This magic formula from the Iroquois, like the Navajo prayer above, accomplishes its purpose in itself. The strength of which the singer stands in need is imparted in the very utterance of his words. The singer not only acknowledges and affirms his strength; indeed he brings it about, he creates it of his own breath; it is done in belief.

The power and beauty of words are sometimes inherent in the most apparently benign and understated utterance, as in this Crow charm, meant to bring sleep upon an enemy:

> At night when we lie down, listening to the wind rustling through the bleached trees, we know not how we get to sleep but we fall asleep, don't we?

or this Chippewa love song:

> *A loon I thought it was*
> *But it was my love's splashing oar.*
> *To Sault Ste. Marie he has departed,*

My love has gone on before me,
Never again can I see him.
A loon I thought it was,
But it was my love's splashing oar.

Among the most succinct and potent of American Indian verbal formulas are the warrior songs.

Let us see, is this real,
Let us see, is this real,
Let us see, is this real,
This life I am living?
Ye gods, who dwell everywhere,
Let us see, is this real,
This life I am living.

This song from the Pawnee is an epitome of the warrior ideal. The singer means to place even his life on the line; if the life he lives is not perfectly real, so seems the consequent meaning, then he had better know it, that he might make a right resolution. It is a moral necessity that he put the matter to the test. There is a quiet irony in this, a rhetorical force that is so closely controlled as to be almost subliminal. The whole formula underscores the quality of life, yet the attitude toward life itself is uncompromisingly rational, the pose nearly indifferent, nearly haughty.

Or this, from the Sioux:

soldiers
you fled
even the eagle dies

In this song we have one of the most concentrated and beautiful examples of American Indian oral tradition that I know. It is a nearly perfect formula; there is only the mysterious equation of soldiers and flight on the one hand and the eagle and death on the other. Yet it is a profound equation in which the eternal elements of life and death and fear are defined in terms of freedom and courage and nobility. One might well brood upon the death of eagles; I have looked at these words on the page a long time, and I have heard them grow up in the silence again and again. They do not fade or fail.

This Sioux formula embodies in seven words the essence of literature, I believe. It is significant that the song was transcribed; that is, it was not composed in writing, but it is preserved on the printed page, it exists now in written form. What was lost or gained in the process of translation and transcription? This we cannot know, but it is perhaps enough to know that the song, as we have it, is alive and powerful and beautiful, and that it is eminently worthy of being preserved for its own sake. It is literature of the highest order.

To Save a Great Vision

I

Several years ago, in Oklahoma, I spent a summer afternoon in the company of a very old and beautiful woman whose name was Ko-sahn. I have written elsewhere* of her and of that afternoon. It was an extraordinary experience for me, one that I know now to have been a high point in my life, a moment of singular honor and privilege and humility. It seemed so at the time, of course, but it seems far more so now; my conviction has deepened steadily over the years. Ko-sahn was a Kiowa, and she was a close friend of my Kiowa grandmother's. Her life was a long one (she was, she reckoned, a hundred years old when I met her); it reached across a whole and crucial period in the history of the Great Plains. She was witness to that history, largely unwritten. She could speak directly from memory of things that had long since passed into legend. There was about her the unmistakable presence of that which is sacred. She was a keeper of the sacred past.

John Neihardt, a renowned poet of the Plains, must also have had the sense that he had entered into the realm of the sacred when he visited Black Elk in May 1931. Earlier, on the occasion of their first meeting, Black Elk had said:

> There is much to teach you. What I know was given to me for men and it is true and it is beautiful. Soon I shall be under the grass and it will be lost. You were sent to save it, and you must come back so that I can teach you.

*in *An American Land Ethic*

Neihardt accepted this trust more than willingly. If the old Sioux holy man's chief purpose was, as he said, to "save his Great Vision for men," Neihardt would be the instrument of preservation. Here is one of the truly fortunate collaborations in our American heritage.

It is through the intercession of John Neihardt, then, that we have access to a principal worldview of the Native American. *Black Elk Speaks*, first published in 1931, is now deservedly recognized as a classic in our high schools and universities. We know this without knowing precisely where to place the book in our traditional categories of learning. Such rubrics as Literature, Anthropology, Folklore, and Religious Studies, not to mention American Studies and Native American Studies, seem equally appropriate frames of reference, immediate contexts. Indeed, the book bears importantly upon all of these and more. But we need not concern ourselves with labels here, any more than we need concern ourselves with the question of authorship or the quality of translation or tran-scription. It is sufficient that *Black Elk Speaks* is an extraordinary human document—and beyond that the record of a spiritual journey, the pil-grimage of a people toward fulfillment, toward the accomplishment of a worthy destiny. That the pilgrimage was in a sense ended at Wounded Knee in 1890, that Black Elk's words at last take a tragic turn—"There is no center any longer, and the sacred tree is dead"—is of little con-sequence in the long run, I believe. For in that sudden and absolute investment in the tragic, in the whole assumption of a tragic sense, there is immeasurable vindication, the achievement of a profound and per-manent dignity.

II

I have stated above that I believe *Black Elk Speaks* is preeminently a human document. By this I mean not that this account tells us of the Oglala Sioux, or even that it reveals to us the extraordinary man Black Elk (or, indeed, that other extraordinary man, Neihardt), but that it tells us of ourselves and of all humankind. I am interested in the universal elements of the narrative, first as an example of oral tradition, then as literature.

Black Elk's account is of course centered in the oral tradition. What does this mean, exactly? It means that the storyteller is illiterate and that his understanding and his use of language are determined by considerations of which we, who function within the written tradition, are at best only vaguely aware. If we are to understand the basic, human elements of Black Elk's account, we must first understand what those considerations are.

Black Elk is a storyteller. I use that term advisedly. In the oral tradition the storyteller is he who takes it upon himself to speak formally, as Black Elk does in this case. He assumes responsibility for his words, for what is created at the level of his human voice. He runs the risk of language, and language is full of risk—it might miscarry, it might be abused in one or more of a thousand ways. His function is essentially creative, inasmuch as language is essentially creative. He creates himself, and his listeners, through the power of his perception, his imagination, his expression. He realizes the power and beauty of language; he believes in the efficacy of words. He is a holy man; his function is sacred.

Perhaps we can better examine these matters if we look at a specific passage. Early on in Black Elk's story he recounts the following:

> It was when I was five years old that my grandfather made me a bow and some arrows. The grass was young and I was on horseback. A thunder storm was coming from where the sun goes down, and just as I was riding into the woods along a creek, there was a kingbird sitting on a limb. This was not a dream, it happened. And I was going to shoot at the kingbird with the bow my grandfather made, when the bird spoke and said: "The clouds all over are one-sided." Perhaps it meant that all the clouds were looking at me. And then it said: "Listen! A voice is calling you! Then I looked up at the clouds, and two men were coming there, headfirst like arrows slanting down; and as they came, they sang a sacred song and the thunder was like

drumming. I will sing it for you. The song and the drumming were like this:

> "Behold, a sacred voice is calling you;
> All over the sky a sacred voice is calling."

I sat there gazing at them, and they were coming from the place where the giant lives (north). But when they were very close to me, they wheeled about toward where the sun goes down, and suddenly they were geese. Then they were gone, and the rain came with a big wind and a roaring.

I did not tell this vision to any one. I liked to think about it, but I was afraid to tell it.

It seems to me that such a passage reflects closely the nature and character of oral tradition, especially American Indian tradition. Taken as a whole, this account appears to be more or less like other vision stories in the same tradition. Let us consider, for the sake of comparison, this somewhat similar Kiowa story:

> Long ago there were bad times. The Kiowas were hungry and there was no food. There was a man who heard his children cry from hunger, and he went out to look for food. He walked four days and became very weak. On the fourth day he came to a great canyon. Suddenly there was thunder and lightning. A voice spoke to him and said, "Why are you following me? What do you want?" The man was afraid. The thing standing before him had the feet of a deer, and its body was covered with feathers. The man answered that the Kiowas were hungry. "Take me with you," the voice said, "and I will give you whatever you want." From that day Tai-me has belonged to the Kiowas.

Both narratives proceed from a cosmology inherent in the Plains culture, a cosmology at the center of which is the Sun Dance. Both narratives proceed then from a vested interest in the so-called Vision Quest—proceed from, perpetuate, and celebrate that ideal. In both narratives the vision (and with it the indivisible voice; we must not lose the force of the oral, audible element) is paramount. In both, that which is seen is strange and unaccountable. And both are extremely portentous. Both accounts are revelations, but what is revealed is suspended in doubt. The meaning of these stories is not to be discovered at once; the quest extends not only to the vision but beyond it to meaning. Finally, both questers after visions are afraid, the one of what he sees, the other to tell of what he has seen. The detail of being afraid underscores the supernatural center of the vision and of its relation in language as well. The vision *and* the story in which it is conveyed are intrinsically powerful.

The Kiowa story is self-contained. Black Elk's account is of course the fragment of a much larger whole. Nevertheless, there is a perceptible integrity even in the fragment and little if any extraneous matter. The implications and consequent meanings of the passage are important. That the gift of a bow and arrow should come from a grandfather, that the arrows should prefigure the two men in the vision, that the sacred voice "all over" the sky which informs the sacred song should anticipate a rainstorm complete with "a big wind and a roaring"—these things are entirely in keeping with both the structure and character of oral tradition.

The attitude of the storyteller toward his story is in the oral tradition appropriately formal. Black Elk stands apart from the story in a sense. He is careful not to intrude upon it. It is not a personal story, not essentially autobiographical; essentially, it is a testament. The telling of the story is a spiritual act, and the storyteller has a profound conviction of the religious dimension in which the act is accomplished.

> You have noticed that everything an Indian does is in a circle, and that is because the Power of the World always works in circles, and everything tries to be round. In the old days when we were a strong and happy people, all our power came to us from the sacred hoop of the nation, and so long as the hoop was unbroken, the people flourished. The flowering tree was the living center of the hoop, and the circle of the four quarters

nourished it. The east gave peace and light, the south gave warmth, the west gave rain, and the north with its cold and mighty wind gave strength and endurance. This knowledge came to us from the outer world with our religion. Everything the Power of the World does is done in a circle. The sky is round, and I have heard that the earth is round like a ball, and so are all the stars. The wind, in its great power, whirls. Birds make their nests in circles, for theirs is the same religion as ours. The sun comes forth and goes down again in a circle. The moon does the same, and both are round. Even the seasons form a great circle in their changing, and always come back again to where they were. The life of a man is a circle from childhood to childhood, and so it is in everything where power moves. Our tepees were round like the nests of birds, and these were always set in a circle, the nation's hoop, a nest of many nests, where the Great Spirit meant for us to hatch our children.

I point to this passage in particular, not only because it is an eloquent explication of the Lakota worldview at its center, but also because it describes the shape of the story itself. Implicit in the passage is the acknowledgment that language, too, is circular. Words follow one upon another, and in the formulation of meaning they return upon themselves. *Black Elk Speaks* is a remarkable example of this principle. It is the circumference of itself; it begins and ends at the same point.

> ... These things I shall remember by the way, and often they may seem to be the very tale itself, as when I was living them in happiness and sorrow. But now that I can see it all as from a lonely hilltop, I know it was the story of a mighty vision given to a man too weak to use it; of a holy tree that should have flourished in a people's heart with flowers and singing birds, and now is withered; and of a people's dream that died in bloody snow.

So is the story begun. And in the end it comes round to this:

I know now then how much was ended then. When I look back now from this high hill of my old age, I can still see the butchered women and children lying heaped and scattered all along the crooked gulch as plain as when I saw them with eyes still young. And I can see that something else died there in the bloody snow and was buried in the blizzard. A people's dream died there. It was a beautiful dream.

And I, to whom so great a vision was given in my youth— you see me now a pitiful old man who has done nothing, for the nation's hoop is broken and scattered. There is no center any longer, and the sacred tree is dead.

Thus there is a consistent symmetry in Black Elk's account. He is at every moment aware of the aesthetic foundation of the storyteller's function. He orders his words. He fashions his language according to ancient conceptions of proportion, design, perspective. The aesthetic realization of his story is not immediately of his own invention; rather, he fits his narrative into the universal scheme. The motion of his voice is the motion of the earth itself.

To the extent that Black Elk re-creates his vision in words, he re-creates himself. He affirms that he has existence in the element of language, and this affirmation is preeminently creative. He declares in effect: *Behold, I give you my vision in these terms, and in the process I give you myself.* In the ultimate achievement of the storyteller's purpose, he projects his spirit into language and therefore beyond the limits of his time and place. It is an act of sheer transcendence. Spiritually he will survive as long as his words survive. He inhabits his vision, and in the telling his vision becomes timeless. The storyteller and the story told are one.

III

John Neihardt was a poet. His poet's sensibility must have made him peculiarly receptive to Black Elk's recitation. Even though he could not understand the language that Black Elk spoke, we cannot doubt, I think, that he discerned quite readily the rhythms, the inflections and alliterations of the holy man's speech. And this discernment is worth a great deal.

> Late in the Moon of the Dark Red Calf or early in the Moon of the Snowblind, Spotted Tail, the Brulé with some others, came to us. His sister was Crazy Horse's mother. He was a great chief and a great warrior before he went over to the Wasichus. I saw him and I did not like him. He was fat with Wasichu food and we were lean with famine.

The quality here is essentially poetic—consider the sustained hissing of the *s*'s throughout, or the alliteration in the final sentence. But I mean not only the immediate quality which informs the translation, but also that fundamental quality which inheres in the substance and integrity of the statement itself. The lyrical names, the precise ordering of detail, the evocation of the warrior ideal, these constitute a kind of common denominator, a bridge between the poem and the song, between literature and legend, between the written tradition and the oral. The transformation of speech into writing—*this* speech into *this* writing—is a matter of great importance, I believe. And Neihardt believed it, too. He brought extraordinary sympathy and dedication to his task.

There are the elements of risk and responsibility here; such is the nature of language. And in the oral tradition these factors are crucial and pervasive. It is a principle of oral tradition that words and the things that are made of words are tentative. A song, or a prayer, or a story, is always but one generation removed from extinction. The risk of loss is constant, therefore, and language is never to be taken for granted. By the same token the storyteller, the man who takes it upon himself to speak, assumes the responsibility of speaking well, of making his words count. The spoken word is the means by which he must keep alive his way of life. There is no other possibility of cultural survival.

I am making the case that a certain spirit of language informs the oral tradition. It is very likely beyond us, who are committed to a written tradition, to say what the spirit of language is, exactly. But in some sense we can bring ourselves to recognize that it exists, and under certain circumstances we can be true to it, more or less. It isn't easy; it requires a remarkable effort and a profound act of the imagination.

John Neihardt was committed to a written tradition, and his commitment was greater than most. He made much good of it in his lifetime. In *Black Elk Speaks*, he exceeds his tradition for a moment. He is made the gift of another man's voice, and he allows us to hear it distinctly, in the realization of meaning.

IV

"My day, I have made it holy."

Like the sun of this song, which sanctifies the day in its light, Black Elk makes holy his story in the telling. The sacred vision is preserved. For this, among other things, we owe to the poet John Neihardt our best thanks.

A First American
Views His Land

First Man
behold:
the earth
glitters
with leaves:
the sky
glistens
with rain.
Pollen
is borne
on winds
that low
and lean
upon
mountains.
Cedars
blacken
the slopes—
and pines.

One hundred centuries ago. There is a wide, irregular landscape in what
is now northern New Mexico. The sun is a dull white disk, low in the
south; it is a perfect mystery, a deity whose coming and going are
inexorable. The gray sky is curdled, and it bears very close upon the
earth. A cold wind runs along the ground, dips and spins, flaking drift
from a pond in the bottom of a ravine. Beyond the wind the silence is

acute. A man crouches in the ravine, in the darkness there, scarcely visible. He moves not a muscle; only the wind lifts a lock of his hair and lays it back along his neck. He wears skins and carries a spear. These things in particular mark his human intelligence and distinguish him as the lord of the universe. And for him the universe is especially *this* landscape; for him the landscape is an element like the air. The vast, virgin wilderness is by and large his whole context. For him there is no possibility of existence elsewhere.

Directly there is a blowing, a rumble of breath deeper than the wind, above him, where some of the hard clay of the bank is broken off and the clods roll down into the water. At the same time there appears on the skyline the massive head of a long-horned bison, then the hump, then the whole beast, huge and black on the sky, standing to a height of seven feet at the hump, with horns that extend six feet across the shaggy crown. For a moment it is poised there; then it lumbers obliquely down the bank to the pond. Still the man does not move, though the beast is now only a few steps upwind. There is no sign of what is about to happen; the beast meanders; the man is frozen in repose.

Then the scene explodes. In one and the same instant the man springs to his feet and bolts forward, his arm cocked and the spear held high, and the huge animal lunges in panic, bellowing, its whole weight thrown violently into the bank, its hooves churning and chipping earth into the air, its eyes gone wide and wild and white. There is a moment in which its awful, frenzied motion is wasted, and it is mired and helpless in its fear, and the man hurls the spear with his whole strength, and the point is driven into the deep, vital flesh, and the bison in its agony staggers and crashes down and dies.

This ancient drama of the hunt is enacted again and again in the landscape. The man is preeminently a predator, the most dangerous of all. He hunts in order to survive; his very existence is simply, squarely established upon that basis. But he hunts also because he can, because he has the means; he has the ultimate weapon of his age, and his prey is plentiful. His relationship to the land has not yet become a moral equation.

But in time he will come to understand that there is an intimate, vital link between the earth and himself, a link that implies an intricate network of rights and responsibilities. In some unimagined future he will understand that he has the ability to devastate and perhaps destroy his environment. That moment will be one of extreme crisis in his evolution.

The weapon is deadly and efficient. The hunter has taken great care in its manufacture, especially in the shaping of the flint point, which is an extraordinary thing. A larger flake has been removed from each face, a groove that extends from the base nearly to the tip. Several hundred pounds of pressure, expertly applied, were required to make these grooves. The hunter, then, is an artisan. His skill, manifest in the manufacture of this artifact, is unsurpassed for its time and purpose. By means of this weapon is the Paleo-Indian hunter eminently able to exploit his environment.

Thousands of years later, about the time that Columbus begins his first voyage to the New World, another man, in the region of the Great Lakes, stands in the forest shade on the edge of a sunlit brake. In a while a deer enters into the pool of light. Silently the man fits an arrow to a bow, draws aim, and shoots. The arrow zips across the distance and strikes home. The deer leaps and falls dead.

But this latter-day man, unlike his ancient predecessor, is only incidentally a hunter; he is also a fisherman, a husbandman, even a physician. He fells trees and builds canoes; he grows corn, squash, and beans, and he gathers fruits and nuts; he uses hundreds of species of wild plants for food, medicine, teas, and dyes. Instead of one animal, or two or three, he hunts many, none to extinction as the Paleo-Indian may have done. He has fitted himself far more precisely into the patterns of the wilderness than did his ancient predecessor. He lives on the land; he takes his living from it; but he does not destroy it. This distinction supports the fundamental ethic that we call conservation today. In principle, if not yet in name, this man is a conservationist.

These two hunting sketches are far less important in themselves than is the long distance between them, the whole possibility within the dimension of time. I believe that in that interim, there grew up in the mind of man an idea of land as sacred.

At dawn
eagles
hie and
hover
above
the plain
where light
gathers
in pools.
Grasses
shimmer
and shine.
Shadows
withdraw
and lie
away
like smoke.

"The earth is our mother. The sky is our father." This concept of nature, which is at the center of the Native American world view, is familiar to us all. But it may well be that we do not understand entirely what the concept is in its ethical and philosophical implications.

I tell my students that the American Indian has a unique investment in the American landscape. It is an investment that represents perhaps thirty thousand years of habitation. That tenure has to be worth something in itself—a great deal, in fact. The Indian has been here a long time; he is at home here. That simple and obvious trust is one of the most important realities of the Indian world, and it is integral in the Indian mind and spirit.

How does such a concept evolve? Where does it begin? Perhaps it begins with the recognition of beauty, the realization that the physical world *is* beautiful. We don't know much about the ancient hunter's sensitivities. It isn't likely that he had leisure in his life for the elaboration of an aesthetic ideal. And yet the weapon he made was beautiful as well as functional. It has been suggested that much of the minute chipping along the edges of his weapon served no purpose but that of aesthetic satisfaction.

A good deal more is known concerning that man of the central forests. He made beautiful boxes and dishes out of elm and birch bark, for example. His canoes were marvelous, delicate works of art. And this aesthetic perception was a principle of the whole Indian world of his time, as indeed it is of our time. The contemporary Native American is a man whose strong aesthetic perceptions are clearly evident in his arts and crafts, in his religious ceremonies, and in the stories and songs of his rich oral tradition. This, in view of the pressures that have been brought to bear upon the Indian world and the drastic changes that have been effected in its landscape, is a blessing and an irony.

Consider for example the Navajos of the Four Corners area where four states converge. In recent years an extensive coal-mining operation has mutilated some of their most sacred land. A large power plant in that same region spews a contamination into the sky that is visible for many miles. And yet, as much as any people of whom I have heard, the Navajos perceive and celebrate the beauty of the physical world.

There is a Navajo ceremonial song that celebrates the sounds that are made in the natural world, the particular voices that beautify the earth:

> *Voice above,*
> *voice of thunder,*
> *speak from the*
> *dark of clouds:*
> *voice below,*
> *grasshopper voice,*
> *speak from the*
> *green of plants;*
> *so may the earth*
> *be beautiful.*

There is in the motion and meaning of this song a comprehension of the world that is peculiarly native, I believe, that is integral in the Native

American mentality. Consider: the singer stands at the center of the natural world, at the source of its sound, of its motion, of its life. Nothing of that world is inaccessible to him or lost upon him. His song is filled with reverence, with wonder and delight, and with confidence as well. He knows something about himself and about the things around him—and he knows that he knows. I am interested in what he sees and hears; I am interested in the range and force of his perception. Our immediate impression may be that his perception is narrow and deep—vertical. After all, "voice above ... voice below," he sings. But is it vertical only? At each level of his expression there is an extension of his awareness across the whole landscape. The voice above is the voice of thunder, and thunder rolls. Moreover, it issues from the impalpable dark clouds and runs upon their horizontal range. It is a sound that integrates the whole of the atmosphere. And even so, the voice below, that of the grasshopper, issues from the broad plain and multiplicity of plants. And of course the singer is mindful of much more than thunder and insects; we are given in his song the wide angle of his vision and his hearing—and we are given the testimony of his dignity, his trust, and his deep belief.

This comprehension of the earth and air is surely a matter of morality, for it brings into account not only man's instinctive reaction to his environment but the full realization of his humanity as well, the achievement of his intellectual and spiritual development as an individual and as a race.

In my own experience I have seen numerous examples of this regard for nature. My grandfather Mammedaty was a farmer in his mature years; his grandfather was a buffalo hunter on the southern plains. It was not easy for Mammedaty to be a farmer; he was a Kiowa, and the Kiowas never had an agrarian tradition. Yet he had to make his living, even if the old, beloved life of roaming the plains and hunting the buffalo was gone forever. So, as much as any man before him, he fitted his mind and will and spirit to the land; there was nothing else. He could not have conceived of living apart from the land.

In *The Way to Rainy Mountain* I set down a small narrative that belongs in the oral tradition of my family. It indicates something essential about the Native American attitude toward the land:

> East of my grandmother's house, south of the pecan grove, there is buried a woman in a beautiful dress. Mammedaty used to know where she is buried, but now no one knows. If you stand on the front porch of the house and look eastward toward Carnegie, you know that the woman is buried somewhere within the range of your vision. But her grave is unmarked. She was buried in a cabinet, and she wore a beautiful dress. How beautiful it was! It was one of those fine buckskin dresses, and it was decorated with elk's teeth and beadwork. That dress is still there, under the ground.

It seems to me that this statement is primarily a declaration of love for the land, in which the several elements—the woman, the dress, and this plain—are at last become one reality, one expression of the beautiful in nature. Moreover, it seems to me a peculiarly Native American expression in this sense: that the concentration of things that are explicitly remembered—the general landscape, the simple, almost abstract nature of the burial, above all the beautiful dress, which is wholly singular (in kind as well as in its function within the narrative)—is especially Indian in character. The things that are *not* explicitly remembered—the woman's name, the exact location of her grave—are the things that matter least in the special view of the storyteller. What matters here is the translation of the woman into the landscape, a translation particularly signified by means of the beautiful and distinctive dress, an *Indian* dress.

In the late 1940s and early 1950s, when I was a boy, I lived for several years at Jemez Pueblo, New Mexico. The Pueblo Indians are perhaps more obviously invested in the land than are other people. Their whole life is predicated upon a thorough perception of the physical world and its myriad aspects. When I first went there to live, the cacique, or chief, of the Pueblos was a venerable old man with long, gray hair and bright, deep-set eyes. He was entirely dignified and imposing—and rather formidable in the eyes of a boy. He excited my imagination a good deal. I was told that this old man kept the calendar of the tribe, that each morning he stood on a certain spot of ground near the center of the town and watched to see where the sun appeared on the skyline. By means of this solar calendar did he know and announce to his people when it was time to plant, to harvest, to perform this or that ceremony. This image of him in my mind's eye—the old man gazing each morning after the ranging sun—came to represent for me the epitome of that real harmony between man and the land that signifies the Indian world.

One day when I was riding my horse along the Jemez River, I looked up to see a long caravan of wagons and people on horseback and on foot. Men, women, and children were crossing the river ahead of me, moving out to the west, where most of the cultivated fields were, the farmland of the town. It was a wonderful sight to see, this long procession, and I was immediately deeply curious. I wanted to investigate, but it was not in me to do so at once, for that racial reserve, that sense of propriety that is deep-seated in Native American culture, stayed me, held me up. Then I saw someone coming toward me on horseback, galloping. It was a friend of mine, a boy of my own age. "Come on," he said. "Come with us." "Where are you going?" I asked casually. But he would not tell me. He simply laughed and urged me to come along, and of course I was very glad to do so. It was a bright spring morning, and I had a good horse under me, and the prospect of adventure was delicious. We moved far out across the eroded plain to the farthest fields at the foot of a great red mesa, and there we planted two large fields of corn. And afterward, on the edge of the fields, we sat on blankets and ate a feast in the shade of a cottonwood grove.

Later I learned it was the cacique's fields we planted. This is an ancient tradition at Jemez. The people of the town plant and tend and harvest the cacique's fields, and in the winter the hunters give him a portion of the meat they bring home from the mountains. It is as if the cacique is himself the translation of man, every man, into the landscape.

I have not forgotten that day, nor shall I forget it. I remember the warm earth of the fields, the smooth texture of seeds in my hands, and the brown water moving slowly and irresistibly among the rows. Above all I remember the spirit in which the procession was made, the work was done, and the feasting was enjoyed. It was a spirit of communion, of the life of each man in relation to the life of the planet and of the infinite distance and silence in which it moves. We made, in concert, an appropriate expression of that spirit.

One afternoon an old Kiowa woman talked to me, telling me of the place in Oklahoma in which she had lived for a hundred years. It was the place in which my grandparents lived, too; and it is the place where I was born. And she told me of a time even further back, when the Kiowas came down from the north and centered their culture in the red earth of the southern plains. She told wonderful stories, and as I listened, I began to feel more and more sure that her voice proceeded from the land itself. I asked her many things concerning the Kiowas, for I wanted to understand all that I could of my heritage. I told the old woman that I had come there to learn from her and from people like her, those in whom the old ways were preserved. And she said simply, "It is good that you have come here." I believe that her word *good* meant many things; for one thing it meant "right," or "appropriate." And indeed it was appropriate that she should speak of the land. She was eminently qualified to do so. She had a great reverence for the land, and an ancient perception of it, a perception that is acquired only in the course of many generations.

It is this notion of the appropriate, along with that of the beautiful, that forms the Native American perspective on the land. In a sense these considerations are indivisible; Native American oral tradition is rich with songs and tales that celebrate natural beauty, the beauty of the natural world. What is more appropriate to our world than that which is beautiful?

> *At noon*
> *turtles*

enter
slowly
into
the warm
dark loam.
Bees hold
the swarm.
Meadows
recede
through planes
of heat
and pure
distance.

Very old in the Native American worldview is the conviction that the earth is vital, that there is a spiritual dimension to it, a dimension in which man rightly exists. It follows logically that there are ethical imperatives in this matter. I think. Inasmuch as I am in the land, it is appropriate that I should affirm myself in the spirit of the land. I shall celebrate my life in the world and the world in my life. In the natural order man invests himself in the landscape and at the same time incorporates the landscape into his own most fundamental experience. This trust is sacred.

The process of investment and appropriation is, I believe, preeminently a function of the imagination. It is accomplished by means of an act of the imagination that is especially ethical in kind. We are what we imagine ourselves to be. The Native American is someone who thinks of himself, imagines himself in a particular way. By virtue of his experience, his idea of himself comprehends his relationship to the land.

And the quality of this imagining is determined as well by racial and cultural experience. The Native American's attitudes toward this landscape have been formulated over a long period of time, a span that reaches back to the end of the Ice Age. The land, *this* land, is secure in his racial memory.

In our society as a whole we conceive of the land in terms of ownership and use. It is a lifeless medium of exchange; it has for most of us, I suspect, no more spirituality than has an automobile, say, or a refrigerator. And our laws confirm us in this view, for we can buy and sell the land, we can exclude each other from it, and in the context of ownership we can use it as we will. Ownership implies use, and use implies consumption.

But this way of thinking of the land is alien to the Indian. His cultural intelligence is opposed to these concepts; indeed, for him they are all but inconceivable quantities. This fundamental distinction is easier to understand with respect to ownership than to use, perhaps. For obviously the Indian does use, and has always used, the land and the available resources in it. The point is that *use* does not indicate in any real way his idea of the land. *Use* is neither his word nor his idea. As an Indian I think, "You say that I use the land, and I reply, yes, it is true; but it is not the first truth. The first truth is that I *love* the land; I see that it is beautiful; I delight in it; I am alive in it."

In the long course of his journey from Asia and in the realization of himself in the New World, the Indian has assumed a deep ethical regard for the earth and sky, a reverence for the natural world that is antipodal to the strange tenet of modern civilization which seemingly has it that man must destroy his environment. It is this ancient ethic of the Native American that must shape our efforts to preserve the earth and the life upon and within it.

> *At dusk*
> *the gray*
> *foxes*
> *stiffen*
> *in cold;*
> *blackbirds*
> *are fixed*
> *in the*
> *branches.*
> *Rivers*

follow
the moon,
the long
white track
of the
full moon.

An American Land Ethic

I

One night a strange thing happened. I had written the greater part of *The Way to Rainy Mountain*—all of it, in fact, except the epilogue. I had set down the last of the old Kiowa tales, and I had composed both the historical and the autobiographical commentaries for it. I had the sense of being out of breath, of having said what it was in me to say on that subject. The manuscript lay before me in the bright light, small, to be sure, but complete; or nearly so. I had written the second of the two poems in which that book is framed. I had uttered the last word, as it were. And yet a whole, penultimate piece was missing. I began once again to write:

> During the first hours after midnight on the morning of November 13, 1833, it seemed that the world was coming to an end. Suddenly the stillness of the night was broken; there were brilliant flashes of light in the sky, light of such intensity that people were awakened by it. With the speed and density of a driving rain, stars were falling in the universe. Some were brighter than Venus; one was said to be as large as the moon.

I went on to say that that event, the falling of the stars on North America, that explosion of Leonid meteors which occurred 137 years ago, is among the earliest entries in the Kiowa calendars. So deeply impressed upon the imagination of the Kiowas is that old phenomenon that it is remembered still; it has become a part of the racial memory.

"The living memory," I wrote, "and the verbal tradition which transcends it, were brought together for me once and for all in the person of Ko-sahn." It seemed eminently right for me to deal, after all, with that old woman. Ko-sahn is among the most venerable people I have ever known. She spoke and sang to me one summer afternoon in Oklahoma. It was like a dream. When I was born she was already old; she was a grown woman when my grandparents came into the world. She sat perfectly still, folded over on herself. It did not seem possible that so many years—a century of years—could be so compacted and distilled. Her voice shuddered, but it did not fail. Her songs were sad. An old whimsy, a delight in language and in remembrance, shone in her one good eye. She conjured up the past, imagining perfectly the long continuity of her being. She imagined the lovely young girl, wild and vital, she had been. She imagined the Sun Dance:

> There was an old, old woman. She had something on her back. The boys went out to see. The old woman had a bag full of earth on her back. It was a certain kind of sandy earth. That is what they must have in the lodge. The dancers must dance upon the sandy earth. The old woman held a digging tool in her hand. She turned towards the south and pointed with her lips. It was like a kiss, and she began to sing:
>
> > *We have brought the earth.*
> > *Now it is time to play;*
> > *As old as I am, I still have the feeling of play.*
>
> That was the beginning of the Sun Dance.

By this time I was back into the book, caught up completely in the act of writing. I had projected myself—imagined myself—out of the room and out of time. I was there with Ko-sahn in the Oklahoma July. We laughed easily together; I felt that I had known her all of my life— all of hers. I did not want to let her go. But I had come to the end. I set down, almost grudgingly, the last sentences:

> It was—all of this and more—a quest, a going forth upon the way to Rainy Mountain. Probably Ko-sahn too is dead now. At

times, in the quiet of evening, I think she must have wondered, dreaming, who she was. Was she become in her sleep that old purveyor of the sacred earth, perhaps, that ancient one who, old as she was, still had the feeling of play? And in her mind, at times, did she see the falling stars?

For some time I sat looking down at these words on the page, trying to deal with the emptiness that had come about inside of me. The words did not seem real. The longer I looked at them, the more unfamiliar they became. At last I could scarcely believe that they made sense, that they had anything whatsoever to do with meaning. In desperation almost, I went back over the final paragraphs, backward and forward, hurriedly. My eyes fell upon the name Ko-sahn. And all at once everything seemed suddenly to refer to that name. The name seemed to humanize the whole complexity of language. All at once, absolutely, I had the sense of the magic of words and of names. Ko-sahn, I said. And I said again, KO-SAHN.

Then it was that that ancient, one-eyed woman stepped out of the language and stood before me on the page. I was amazed, of course, and yet it seemed to me entirely appropriate that this should happen.

"Yes, grandson," she said. "What is it? What do you want?"

"I was just now writing about you," I replied, stammering. "I thought—forgive me—I thought that perhaps you were . . . That you had . . ."

"No," she said. And she cackled. And she went on. "You have imagined me well, and so I am. You have imagined that I dream, and so I do. I have seen the falling stars."

"But all of this, this *imagining*," I protested, "this has taken place—is taking place in my mind. You are not actually here, not here in this room." It occurred to me that I was being extremely rude, but I could not help myself. She seemed to understand.

"Be careful of your pronouncements, grandson," she answered. "You imagine that I am here in this room, do you not? This is worth something. You see, I have existence, whole being, in your imagination. It is but one kind of being, to be sure, but it is perhaps the best of all kinds. If I am not here in this room, grandson, then surely neither are you."

"I think I see what you mean," I said. I felt justly rebuked. "Tell me grandmother, how old are you?"

"I do not know," she replied. "There are times when I think that I am the oldest woman on earth. You know, the Kiowas came into the world through a hollow log. In my mind's eye I have seen them emerge, one by one, from the mouth of the log. I have seen them so clearly, how they were dressed, how delighted they were to see the world around them. I *must* have been there. And I must have taken part in that old migration of the Kiowas from the Yellowstone to the southern plains, for I have seen antelope bounding in the tall grass near the Big Horn River, and I have seen the ghost forests in the Black Hills. Once I saw the red cliffs of Palo Duro Canyon. I was with those who were camped in the Wichita Mountains when the stars fell."

"You are indeed very old," I said, "and you have seen many things."

"Yes, I imagine that I have," she replied. Then she turned slowly around, nodding once, and receded into the language I had made. And then I imagined I was alone in the room.

II

Once in his life a man ought to concentrate his mind upon the remembered earth, I believe. He ought to give himself up to a particular landscape in his experience, to look at it from as many angles as he can, to wonder about it, to dwell upon it. He ought to imagine that he touches it with his hands at every season and listens to the sounds that are made upon it. He ought to imagine the creatures there and all the faintest motions of the wind. He ought to recollect the glare of noon and all the colors of the dawn and dusk.

The Wichita Mountains rise out of the southern plains in a long crooked line that runs from east to west. The mountains are made of red earth, and of rock that is neither red nor blue but some very rare admixture of the two, like the feathers of certain birds. They are not so high and mighty as the mountains of the Far West, and they bear a different relationship to the land around them. One does not imagine that they are distinctive in themselves, or indeed that they exist apart from the plain in any sense. If you try to think of them in the abstract, they lose the look of mountains. They are preeminently an expression of the larger landscape, more perfectly organic than one can easily imagine. To behold these mountains from the plain is one thing; to see the plain from the mountains is something else. I have stood on the top of Mount Scott and seen the earth below, bending out into the whole circle of the sky. The wind runs always close upon the slopes, and there are times when you hear the rush of it like water in the ravines.

Here is the hub of an old commerce. More than a hundred years ago the Kiowas and Comanches journeyed outward from the Wichitas in every direction, seeking after mischief and medicine, horses and hostages. Sometimes they went away for years, but they always returned, for the land had got hold of them. It is a consecrated place, and even now there is something of the wilderness about it. There is a game preserve in the hills. Animals graze away in the open meadows or, closer by, keep to the shadows of the groves: antelope and deer, longhorns and buffalo. It was here, the Kiowas say, that the first buffalo came into the world.

The yellow grassy knoll that is called Rainy Mountain lies a short distance to the north and west. There, on the west side, is the ruin of an old school where my grandmother went as a wild girl in blanket and braids to learn of numbers and of names in English. And there she is buried.

> Most is your name the name of this dark stone.
> Deranged in death, the mind to be inheres
> Forever in the nominal unknown,
> The wake of nothing audible he hears
> Who listens here and now to hear your name.

The early sun, red as a hunter's moon,
Runs in the plain. The mountain burns and shines;
And silence is the long approach of noon
Upon the shadow that your name defines——
And death this cold, black density of stone.

III

I am interested in the way that a man looks at a given landscape and takes possession of it in his blood and brain. For this happens, I am certain, in the ordinary motion of life. None of us lives apart from the land entirely; such an isolation is unimaginable. We have sooner or later to come to terms with the world around us—and I mean especially the physical world, not only as it is revealed to us immediately through our senses, but also as it is perceived more truly in the long turn of seasons and of years. And we must come to moral terms. There is no alternative, I believe, if we are to realize and maintain our humanity, for our humanity must consist in part in the ethical as well as in the practical ideal of preservation. And particularly here and now is that true. We Americans need now more than ever before—and indeed more than we know—to imagine who and what we are with respect to the earth and sky. I am talking about an act of the imagination, essentially, and the concept of an American land ethic.

It is no doubt more difficult to imagine the landscape of America now, than it was in, say, 1900. Our whole experience as a nation in this century has been a repudiation of the pastoral ideal which informs so much of the art and literature of the nineteenth century. One effect of the technological revolution has been to uproot us from the soil. We have become disoriented, I believe; we have suffered a kind of psychic dislocation of ourselves in time and space. We may be perfectly sure of where we are in relation to the supermarket and the next coffee break, but I doubt that any of us knows where he is in relation to the stars and to the solstices. Our sense of the natural order has become dull and unreliable. Like the wilderness itself, our sphere of instinct has diminished in proportion as we have failed to imagine truly what it is. And yet I believe that it is possible to formulate an ethical idea of the land—a notion of what it is and must be in our daily lives—and I believe moreover that it is absolutely necessary to do so.

It would seem on the surface of things that a land ethic is something that is alien to, or at least dormant in, most Americans. Most of us have developed an attitude of indifference toward the land. In terms of my own experience, it is difficult to see how such an attitude could ever have come about.

IV

Ko-sahn could remember where my grandmother was born. "It was just there," she said, pointing to a tree, and the tree was like a hundred others that grew up in the broad depression of the Washita River. I could see nothing to indicate that anyone had ever been there, spoken so much as a word, or touched the tips of his fingers to the tree. But in her memory Ko-sahn could see the child. I think she must have remembered my grandmother's voice, for she seemed for a long moment to listen and to hear. There was a still, heavy heat upon that place; I had the sense that ghosts were gathering there.

And in the racial memory, Ko-sahn had seen the falling stars. For her there was no distinction between the individual and the racial experience, even as there was none between the mythical and the historical. Both were realized for her in the one memory, and that was of the land. This landscape, in which she had lived for a hundred years, was the common denominator of everything that she knew and would ever know—and her knowledge was profound. Her roots ran deep into the earth, and from those depths she drew strength enough to hold still against all the forces of chance and disorder. And she drew therefrom the sustenance of meaning and of mystery as well. The falling stars were not for Ko-sahn an isolated or accidental phenomenon. She had a great personal investment in that awful commotion of light in the night sky. For it remained to be imagined. She must at last deal with it in words; she must appropriate it to her understanding of the whole universe. And, again, when she spoke of the Sun Dance, it was an essential expression of her relationship to the life of the earth and to the sun and moon.

In Ko-sahn and in her people we have always had the example of a deep, ethical regard for the land. We had better learn from it. Surely that ethic is merely latent in ourselves. It must now be activated, I believe. We Americans must come again to a moral comprehension of the earth and air. We must live according to the principle of a land ethic. The alternative is that we shall not live at all.

On Indian-White Relations: A Point of View

From time to time I have been asked to identify and explain, within a brief space, what I consider to be the most crucial, most vital issue at work in the past five hundred years of North American Indian and white relations. That is a very tall order, of course, and a very serious matter. I can only respond in a personal and a straightforward way.

I believe that there is a fundamental dichotomy at the center of these relations, past and present. The Indian and the white man perceive the world in different ways. I take it that this is an obvious fact and a foregone conclusion. But at the same time I am convinced that we do not understand the distinction entirely or even sufficiently. I myself do not understand it sufficiently, but I may be more acutely aware of it by virtue of my experience than are most. Let me qualify my point of view on the subject in order that my remarks may be taken within a certain frame of reference. I am an Indian. I was born into the Indian world, and I have lived a good part of my life in that world. That is worth something, and it is an indispensable consideration in the argument I wish to develop here. You may recall that Oliver La Farge, in discussing his own, narrative point of view in the novel *Laughing Boy* (1929), drew a distinction between "the thing observed and the thing experienced." La Farge correctly thought of himself as an observer; his point of view was removed from the experience of which he wrote, and the distance of that remove was and is finally immeasurable. That is not to say that his powers of observation were in any way deficient—far from it; nor is it to say that *Laughing Boy* is less than a distinguished work of art. It is merely to remark the existence of intrinsic variables in man's perception of his universe, variables that are determined to some real extent on the basis of his genetic constitution. In the case of my own writing, where it centers upon Indian life, and especially upon an Indian way of looking at the world, I can say with some validity, I think, that I have written of "the thing experienced" as well as of "the thing observed." What this may or may not mean in terms of literary advantage is not a question that I wish to raise here, however. For the time being it is enough to establish that such a distinction is *prima facie* real, and it bears importantly upon the matter under discussion.

What of the dichotomy that I have mentioned? How can we get at it? Let me suppose that my daughter, Lore, comes to me with the question, "Where does the sun live?" In my middle-aged and "educated" brain I consider the possibilities of reply. I begin to construct a formula like this: "Well, darling, as you can see, the sun lives in the sky." But already another perception, deeper in the blood, leads me to say, "The sun lives in the earth." I am aware that the first answer is more acceptable to the logic of my age than is the second, and it is more congenial to my learning. The sun is to be observed in the sky and not elsewhere. We are taught beyond any possibility of doubt that the sun and the earth are separated by an all but unimaginable distance. The word *live* we grant to the child as an indulgence, if we grant it at all; it is a metaphor, merely. We certainly do not mean to say that the sun is alive. We mean that from our point of view the visible sun has its place in the heavens. And we take it for granted that we are speaking of dead matter. But the first answer is not true to my experience, my deepest, oldest experience, the memory in my blood.

For to the Indian child who asks the question, the parent replies, "The sun lives in the earth." The sun-watcher among the Rio Grande Pueblos, whose sacred task it is to observe, each day, the very point of the sun's emergence on the skyline, knows in the depths of his being that the sun is alive and that it is indivisible with the earth, and he refers to the farthest eastern mesa as "the sun's house." The Jemez word for home, *ketha'ame,* bears critical connotations of belonging. Should someone say to the sun, "Where are you going?" the sun would surely answer, "I am going home," and it is understood at once that home is the earth. All things are alive in this profound unity in which are all elements, all animals, all things. One of the most beautiful of Navajo prayers begins *"Tsegi yei!* House made of dawn..." And my father remembered that, as a boy, he had watched with wonder and something like fear the old man Koi-khan-hodle, "Dragonfly," stand in the first light, his arms outstretched and his painted face fixed on the east, and "pray the sun out of the ground." His voice, for he prayed aloud, struck at the great, misty silence of the plains morning, entered into it, carried through it to the rising sun. His words made one of the sun and earth, one of himself and the boy who watched, one of the boy and generations to come. Even now, along an arc of time, that man appears to me, and his voice takes hold of me. There is no sunrise without Koi-khan-hodle's prayer.

I want to indicate as best I can an American Indian attitude (for want of a better word) toward the world as a whole. It is an attitude that involves the fullest accomplishment of belief. And I am talking neither about philosophy nor religion; I am talking about a spiritual sense so ancient as to be primordial, so pervasive as to be definitive—not an idea, but a perception on the far side of ideas, an act of understanding as original and originative as the Word. The dichotomy that most closely informs the history of Indian-white relations is realized in language, I believe.

Much has been said and written concerning the Indian's conception of time. Time is a wonderful abstraction; the only way in which we can account for apparent change in our world is by means of the concept of time. The language in which I write and you read upon this page is predicated upon a familiar system of tenses—past, present, and future. In our Western understanding of time we involve the correlative of distance. The past is away in that direction, the future in that, and the present is just here, where I happen to be. But we speak of the passage of time; times come and go, the day will come. We remain in place and observe the flow of time, just as we sit at the cinema and watch, fascinated, as images fly before our eyes. The plane of time is shattered; it is composed of moments, *ad infinitum*, in perpetual motion.

"He loved melons. Always, when we went in the wagon to Carnegie, we stopped at a certain place, a place where there was a big tree. And we sat in the shade there and ate melons. I was little, but I remember. He loves melons, and he always stops at that place." When my father spoke to me of my grandfather, who died before I was born, he invariably slipped into the present tense. And this is a common thing in my experience of the Indian world. For the Indian there is something like an extended present. Time as motion is an illusion; indeed, time itself is an illusion. In the deepest sense, according to the native perception, there is only the dimension of timelessness, and in that dimension all things happen.

The earth confirms this conviction in calendars of "geologic time." Colin Fletcher wrote a book in which he described his walk through the Grand Canyon. It was called significantly, *The Man Who Walked Through Time*. In Fletcher's title we come as close as we can, perhaps, to one of the absolutes of the Indian world. If you stand on the edge of Monument Valley and look across space to the great monoliths that stand away in the silence, you will understand how it is that the mind of man can grasp the notion of eternity. At some point along the line of your sight there is an end of time, and you see beyond into timelessness.

> *as my eyes*
> *search*
> *the prairie*
> *I feel the summer*
> *in the spring*

In this Chippewa song, time is reduced to a profound evanescence. We are given a stillness like that of the stars.

Yvor Winters, who was my teacher and my friend, wrote in the introduction to his final work, *Forms of Discovery*, "Unless we understand the history which produced us, we are determined by that history; we may be determined in any event, but the understanding gives us a chance." It is a provocative, even compelling statement. And it is eminently wise. But, with respect to our present discussion, there arises the question, How are we to understand the meaning of the word *history?*

In the summer of the centennial year, 1876, General George A. Custer and 265 men of the Seventh Cavalry were killed at the Battle of the Little Bighorn in Montana. Rutherford B. Hayes and Samuel J. Tilden were nominated by their respective parties for the office of President of the United States. Colorado was admitted to the Union. *The Chicago Daily News* was founded, and the Dewey Decimal System was originated.

The summer of 1876 is indicated on the calendar of Set-t'an (a Kiowa) by the rude drawing of a medicine lodge, below which are the tracks of horses. This was the "Sun Dance when Sun-boy's horses were stolen." During the dance, which was held that year at the fork of the Red River and Sweetwater Creek, all of Sun-boy's horses were stolen by a band of Mexicans. Following the dance a war party was sent in pursuit of the thieves, but the horses were not recovered. This is the single record of the summer of that year.

Set-t'an understood history in what can only seem to us extraordinary and incongruous terms. The summer of 1876 was in his mind forever to be identified with the theft of horses. You and I can marvel at that, but we cannot know what the loss of a horse meant to Set-t'an or to his people, whose culture is sometimes called the "horse" culture or the "centaur" culture. We can try to imagine; we can believe that Set-t'an was as deeply concerned to understand the history that produced him as any man can be. My friend Dee Brown wrote in 1966 an estimable study of the year 1876, which he called *The Year of the Century*. Consider that, in some equation that we have yet to comprehend fully, Brown's book is more or less equal to a simple pictograph, the barest of line drawings, on a hide painting of the nineteenth century—or the wall of an ancient cave.

We could go on with such comparisons as these, but this much will serve, I think, as a basis for the main point I wish to make. A good deal has been written about the inequities which inform the history of Indian-white relations in this country, by far the greater part of it from the point of view of the white man, of course. This is the point of view that has been—that can be—articulated in terms that are acceptable to American society as a whole, after all. One of the most perplexing ironies of American history is the fact that the Indian has been effectively silenced by the intricacies of his own speech, as it were. Linguistic diversity has been a formidable barrier to Indian-white diplomacy. And underlying this diversity is again the central dichotomy, the matter of a difference in ways of seeing and making sense of the world around us.

The American Indian has a highly developed oral tradition. It is in the nature of oral tradition that it remains relatively constant; languages are slow to change for the reason that they represent a greater investment on the part of society. One who has only an oral tradition thinks of language in this way: my words exist at the level of my voice. If I do not speak with care, my words are wasted. If I do not listen with care, words are lost. If I do not remember carefully, the very purpose of words is frustrated. This respect for words suggests an inherent morality in man's understanding and use of language. Moreover, that moral comprehension is everywhere evident in American Indian speech. On the other hand, the written tradition tends to encourage an indifference to language. That is to say, writing produces a false security where our attitudes toward language are concerned. We take liberties with words; we become blind to their sacred aspect.

By virtue of the authority vested in me by section 465 of the Revised Statutes (25 U.S.C. #9 [section 9 of this title]) and as President of the United States, the Secretary of Interior is hereby designated and empowered to exercise, without the approval, ratification, or other action of the President or of any other officer of the United States, any and all authority conferred upon the United States by section 403 (a) of the Act of April 11, 1968, 82 Stat. 79 (25 U.S.C. #1323 (a) [subsec. (a) of this section]): provided, That acceptance of retrocession of all or any measure of civil or criminal jurisdiction, or both, by the Secretary hereunder shall be effected by publication in the *Federal Register* of a notice which shall specify the jurisdiction retroceded and the effective date of the retrocession: Provided further, That acceptance of such retrocession of criminal jurisdiction shall be effected only after consultation by the Secretary with the Attorney General.

Executive Order No. 11435, 1968

I have heard that you intend to settle us on a reservation near the mountains. I don't want to settle. I love to roam over the prairies. There I feel free and happy, but when we settle down we grow pale and die. I have laid aside my lance, bow, and shield, and yet I feel safe in your presence. I have told the truth. I have no little lies hid about me, but I don't know how it is with the commissioners. Are they as clear as I am?

Satanta, Kiowa chief

The examples above speak for themselves. The one is couched in the legal diction of a special parlance, one that is far removed from our general experience of language. Its meaning is obscure; the words themselves seem to stand in the way of meaning. The other is in the plain style, a style that preserves, in its way, the power and beauty of language. In the historical relationship in question, the language of diplomacy has been determined by the considerations that have evolved into the style of the first of these examples. It is far removed from the American Indian oral tradition, far from the rhythms of oratory and storytelling and song.

This fundamental difference in ways of looking at the world, as those differences are reflected in the language of diplomacy, seems to me to constitute the most important issue in Indian-white relations in the past five hundred years.

The Morality of Indian Hating

In the winter of 1833 the Kiowas were camped on Elm Fork, a branch of the Red River west of the Wichita Mountains. In the preceding summer they had suffered a massacre at the hands of the Osages, and Tai-me, the sacred Sun Dance doll and most powerful medicine of the tribe, had been stolen. At no time in the history of their migration from the north, and in the evolution of their plains culture, had the Kiowas been more vulnerable to despair. The loss of Tai-me was a deep psychological wound. In the early cold of November 13 there occurred over North America an explosion of meteors. The Kiowas were awakened by the sterile light of falling stars, and they ran out into the false day and were terrified.

The year the stars fell is among the earliest entries in the Kiowa calendars, and it is permanent in the Kiowa mind. There was symbolic meaning in that November sky. With the coming of natural dawn there began a new and darker age for the Kiowa people; the last culture to evolve on this continent began to decline. Within four years of the falling stars the Kiowas signed their first treaty with the government; within twenty, four major epidemics of smallpox and Asiatic cholera destroyed more than half their number; and within scarcely more than a generation their horses were taken from them and the herds of buffalo were slaughtered and left to waste upon the plains.

It is expedient to begin with a particular people and a symbolic event. In a certain sense it is also necessary; one is obliged, by the nature of the subject, to focus upon particulars and their symbols. The unique position of the Indian in this society is anomalously fixed and mutable, here and there, truth and fiction. The Indian has been for a long time generalized in the imagination of the white man. Denied the acknowledgment of individuality and change, he has been made to become in theory what he could not become in fact, a synthesis of himself. This is not semantic trickery. The Navajo, to illustrate, is an American Indian, but "the American Indian" is not conversely a Navajo; he is rather, to the public mind, that lonely specter who stood for two hundred years in the way of civilization, who was removed time and again by force, and who was given in defeat that compensation we call savage nobility, after the example of Rousseau.

The persistent attempt to generalize the Indian has resulted in a delusion and a nomenclature of half truths. The so-called Indian problem is impossible to define. The term is furthermore misleading and dangerous, for it holds up the attractive suggestion that there is *one* problem and, by implication therefore, *one* solution. The suggestion is naive and fallacious, of course; yet it has been the basis of a historical diplomacy. Federal management of Indian affairs has always been expressed in general and uniform policy. Predictably that policy has had but slight and accidental relevance to a random majority of the Indian people and none at all to a struggling, perhaps desperate, minority. Diversity is the principal barrier in the way of cultural assimilation; it will continue to be a barrier for generations to come. There are several hundred societies of Indians. Our reservations now support, with bare adequacy, nearly four hundred thousand inhabitants. And there are more than a hundred living Indian languages.

The history of Indian-white relations conforms to a pattern which has come to be associated with the evolution of the democratic faith: a geographical expansion from east to west and a succession of events which mark the development of American nationalism from the seventeenth century to the twentieth. The outlines of that pattern form the character of my own ideas on the subject of Indian cultural integration, and throughout this essay I shall hold a part of my attention on them for the sake of perspective. There is a meaningful symmetry in the shape of the past. More important than the tangible history of Indian-white relations, however, is the interaction of ideas and attitudes which inform that relationship and transcend it. Those ideas and attitudes are, on both sides, matters of morale and morality.

The military campaigns which were waged on the receding frontier of the last century were less consequential by far than was the intrusion of the white man's "civilization" upon the sanctity of the red man's faith. The Indian can recognize and understand malice, and he can bear pain with legendary self-possession. What he can neither recognize nor understand is that particular atmosphere of moral and ideological ambiguity in which the white man prevails, a traditional milieu which is characterized in part by a sense of finality in thought, an immediacy in judgment, and a general preoccupation with efficiency.

Implicit in these characteristics is the inclination to impose the most convenient identities upon friends and acquaintances, strangers and enemies. The Indian has been compelled to make his way under an imposed identity of defeat. He has been made to live for a long time with the conviction—now indivisibly his and the white man's—that the best possessions of his mind and soul are inane. Moralities can be violated and destroyed. Moral degeneration is conceived in guilt and nurtured in prejudice. It is among the most hideous of psychological deformities, and it perpetuates itself in its own infection. The Indian has been afflicted with that for which society prescribes neither prevention nor cure.

In 1705 there appeared an American book entitled *History of the Present State of Virginia* in which the author, Robert Beverly, described the contemporary circumstances of the Virginia Indians in these words:

> They have on several accounts reasons to lament the arrival of
> the Europeans, by whose means they seem to have have lost
> their Felicity, as well as their Innocence. The *English* have taken
> away great part of their Country and consequently made every-
> thing less plenty amongst them. They have introduced Drunk-
> enness and Luxury amongst them, which have multiply'd their
> Wants, and put them upon desiring a thousand things, they
> never dreamt of before.

The rule of convenience had begun already to enchant the neolithic mind. It is an unbroken spell; in the nearly three centuries since Beverly made his observation, the Indians have regained neither felicity nor innocence, and time has brought them new reasons to lament.

Colonel John Moredock of Illinois, whose story is related indirectly by Melville in *The Confidence Man,* was one who, even in the nineteenth century, had outlived his cause. The Indian hater is no more current than are the atrocities upon which he fed. Yet the particular morality of which Moredock is the spokesman is a cornerstone in the Puritan ethic.

The relationship between the white man and the red was doomed from the outset by a conflict of attitudes and a disposition of intolerance. The initial experience of that relationship was agitated by the cross-purposes of European imperial design. The immediate problems which arose out of colonial establishment are, with reference to the Indian, the common denominators of subsequent history: the question of Indian ownership of land, the development of natural resources, and an uncompromising determination on the part of the white man either to "civilize" the Indian or to eliminate him.

Even so, there was no unanimity in the white man's approach. The Spanish were committed to a system of feudalism; the French were concerned chiefly to exploit the economics of the fur trade; and the English were bound to an agrarian tradition. From the Indian point of view, history has resolved this plurality of interests with a sad significance. It was the English who prevailed in the New World, and it was they whose temperament could concede no usefulness to the Indian. The motives of Spanish and French settlement were sufficiently international in kind to encourage and to realize cooperation. The Indian could be useful to both nations in America; and at the same time, he was well suited to serfdom, and he knew no peer as a hunter. In the New World colonies of France and Spain, therefore, there was no alternative to joint occupation of the land. The Indian was invited to participate in the colonial enterprise, and his participation extended to, and included, intermarriage. But the English could respect the Indian neither as hind nor hunter. Indeed, he was worse than useless; he was an impediment.

The moral aspect of the confrontation between Puritan and Indian is given sharp relief in the context of intercultural relations by the very nature of Calvinism itself and by the sometimes sudden and violent actualities of history. Such an actuality was the so-called Pequod War, of which many have doubtless heard, but of which very few know the causes and effects. It is no wonder. The war is of little historical significance in itself; but, in symbolic terms, it represents a moral precedent upon which a tradition of oppression has been based.

The Pequods were a weak branch of the Algonquin stock which had been severed and driven to the sea by an old warfare with the powerful Iroquois nation. In 1637 the Pequods elected to defend the rich Connecticut Valley against the encroachment of white settlement. Moreover, they threatened to make good their resistance by creating a confederation of local tribes. They were on the point of forming an alliance with the Narragansetts when the recollection of ancient enmities made them pause.

Taking full advantage of the hesitation, the English moved swiftly against the Pequods in a campaign that virtually exterminated the entire tribe. The colonists surprised the Indian stronghold at Fort Mystic in modern-day Connecticut and burned it to the ground. In just more than an hour, some six hundred Indians were shot or burned to death. The English lost two men in the encounter. The grim business of annihilation went on. There began a relentless pursuit of the Pequod survivors. Homeless and grieving, they were easily found and destroyed.

The devastation of the Pequods was a triumph of the Puritan spirit. There was celebration in the New England towns, and the Reverend Cotton Mather called upon his congregation to thank God that "on this day we have sent six hundred heathen souls to hell."

A historian of the Pequod War wrote in 1910:

> No comment which analysts of later times might attempt could possibly compass the vindictiveness of the English upon this occasion. The only palliation available to the historian recording these transactions is to imagine himself surrounded with the perils which menaced the meager population of the English at

that time...If one could imagine himself in a wilderness of woods beset by a pack of hungry wolves he might better appreciate the situation...It is barely possible that in the consummation of these killings of the Pequods the intolerancy of the Puritan found a natural vent, and that he carried on this work with a grim satisfaction.

There is a curious and troubled indecision behind these words. The historian is bending under the weight of an old and malignant confusion of attitudes and loyalties. In the same breath he deplores and defends the morality in which his own prejudices have their roots. He is eminently honest, but he cannot be objective. The story he is concerned to tell has become in his own mind the parable of the solitary man and the hungry wolves. His dilemma is one that concerns us all.

A final word on the Pequod War. The Pequods were one of the few peoples who were undiminished by a plague which ravaged the entire coastal plain from Connecticut to Maine in the decade preceding the founding of Plymouth Plantation. It has been estimated that two thirds of all the inhabitants of that region were consumed by pestilence between the years 1613 and 1618. The white men who subsequently touched upon that land were peculiarly alert to the signs of providence. It was their mandate to secure against all impediments the indulgence of an angry and merciless God. They recognized at once their Old Testament foe in the New World wilderness; the Fiend was everywhere present in the painted faces which peered from behind the trees and in the suspicious forms which strode noiselessly over the brittle leaves. The Indian was one whose very existence opposed the will of God; so much was made certain by the fact that God had visited a contagion upon the savage race. He had cleared the way for his faithful and enlightened few through the agency of disease.

That conviction, refined and fortified by such historical phenomena as the Pequod War, made once and for all unacceptable Roger Williams's queer notion of giving value for Indian land, of purchasing that land, as in Europe, however foreign that notion would have been to the inhabitants of the so-called New World. Implicit in that conviction are two assumptions which have acquired the status of truth in this society. One is the assumption, already expressed, that the Indian is an impediment to the progress of civilization; the other is the related assumption that the rights, both natural and legal, which dignify the white man are unavailable to the Indian. The particular morality which can accommodate these ideas is pragmatic and malleable rather than ideal and absolute. It is the morality (to borrow the juxtaposition made famous by Henry Adams) of the dynamo rather than that of the Virgin. It is relevant to the present context that the assumptions here specified suggest a kind of logical syllogism the conclusion of which is a condition of intolerance and aversion. Whatever else he might have been, Colonel Moredock of Illinois was a man who came honestly by his bias.

The Kiowas who watched the strange commotion of the stars on the morning of November 13, 1833, were a people whose way of life was relatively new. It was a good life, for it enabled the Kiowas to possess dignity and well-being. In order to understand what happened to the Kiowas when their way of life was destroyed, it is necessary to raise an old religion from the dead. There are two legends in the unwritten literature of the Kiowa people which I shall recount. They are brief, and they will give emphasis to certain points I wish later to make.

The first is the story of the man who found Tai-me:

> Long ago there were bad times. The Kiowas were hungry and there was no food. There was a man who heard his children cry from hunger, and he began to search for food. He walked four days and became very weak. On the fourth day he came to a great canyon. Suddenly there was thunder and lightning. A Voice spoke to him and said, "Why are you following me? What do you want?" The man was afraid. The thing standing before him had the feet of a deer, and its body was covered with feathers. The man answered that the Kiowas were hungry. "Take me with you," the Voice said, "and I will give you whatever you want." From that day Tai-me has belonged to the Kiowas.

The second legend is that of two warrior brothers:

On a raid against the Utes, one of two Kiowa brothers was captured. The other stole into the Ute camp and tried to set his brother free, but he too was captured. The chief of the Utes had respect for the man's bravery, and he made a bargain with him. If he could carry his brother on his back and walk upon a row of greased buffalo heads without falling to the ground, both brothers would be given horses and allowed to return in safety to their home. The man bore his brother on his back and walked upon the heads of the buffalo and kept his footing. The Ute chief was true to his word, and the Kiowa brothers returned to their people on horseback.

I relate these stories not only because they are eloquent and venerable but also because they express the truest response to being that man can make. That is their essential value. They are the true reflections of that response, that most moral of human acts. These particular legends grow out of different times and experiences, and they reveal different ways of thinking.

Tai-me came to the Kiowas as they were about to enter upon the southern plains. They had no horses, and they were preoccupied with the simple problem of survival. Their culture was based upon the principle of mobility, and they followed the herds of animals which grazed upon a seemingly boundless expanse of land. They knew no better than to hunt on foot with crude weapons. When they found rare moments in which to explain their world to themselves, they did so in terms of suffering and hope. The Tai-me myth is not an entertainment, nor even the journal of an old salvation; it is infinitely more. It is an emotional reaction to the elemental experience of being, the affirmation of an eternal reality behind all appearances; it is sacred.

But, in itself, myth is an inadequate expression of the human spirit. Ritual, that ancient effort of man to fashion his very bone and muscle into essential prayer, enabled the Kiowas to have existence in a world that was beyond the capacity of the senses to perceive. With Tai-me came the Sun Dance religion.

When my father was a boy, an old man used to come to the house which my grandfather built near Rainy Mountain Creek. He was a lean old man in braids and was impressive in his age and bearing. His English name was Cheyney. Every morning, my father tells me, Cheyney would paint his wrinkled face, go out, and pray aloud to the rising sun. I like to hear of that old man. I like to watch him make his prayer with the eyes of my mind, though I am nearly ashamed to intrude upon his privacy. Old man Cheyney had come to terms with himself and the world. He did not for a moment doubt the source of his strength, and each morning he returned to it his wonder and his words.

The earth where Cheyney prayed is a deep red, and it bears the innumerable wounds of erosion. It is a huge land—so huge that only sound can possess it; a single tree can dominate the plain, but nothing can fill it. It is the kind of landscape in which a man is seen always against the sky—and a man on the back of a horse is regal. The air is hot and clear and filled with an essence that qualifies all objects in the eye and ear. There, in early summer, I have seen the sun rise out of the ground an immense red-orange disk, scarcely brighter than the moon, beautiful and strange and health-giving. It was old man Cheyney's god.

The Sun Dance was the great medicine dance of the Kiowas. It was held at least once each year at a time and place designated by the Tai-me keeper. All the bands of the tribe converged upon the Sun Dance place and camped in the presence of the great ancestral medicine. The institution of the Sun Dance was a concerted expression of tribal integrity. As a social event it was a time for the exchange of gossip and wares, an opportunity to show off prize possessions, a festive occasion upon which to take stock of blood resources and prospects.

But the Sun Dance was preeminently an act of faith. It restored power to the people; it invested them with purpose, thus dignity and strength; it enabled them for a moment to partake of divinity, to send their voices—however frail—against the silence at the edge of the world. During the dance Tai-me was exposed to view. It was suspended from a branch of the sacred tree in the Sun Dance lodge. The rest of the time it was—and is now—kept in parfleche which is wrapped in a blanket and bound with strips of ticking. The Sun Dance lasted four days and nights. A buffalo bull was killed, its hide draped on the limbs of the sacred tree and its head impaled at the top. The buffalo was from the beginning the thread of life; it was food and shelter, god and beast. The head of a buffalo bull, uppermost on the Tai-me tree, its dead eyes fixed on the skyline to the east, was the symbol of life itself. And nothing could have been more perfectly symbolic. The Kiowas could have conceived of no greater sacrifice. The principal dancers fasted the four days through and danced to the edge of exhaustion. Paintings of the sun and moon were made on their bodies, and later the flesh was cut away so that the images were permanent. But the dancers were not bled; they were not made to endure torture as were the dancers of certain other tribes on the plains. Far more intimately than we can easily imagine, the Kiowas bound themselves to their religion. Their commitment to faith and morality was total and deliberate. Though the Sun Dance became the supreme religious institution of a young and short-lived culture, it was unspeakably old in itself—as old as the need of man to know his god.

The Sun Dance died away because the white man forbade it and because the white man destroyed the buffalo. The last Kiowa Sun Dance was held in 1887 on a tributary of the Washita river above Rainy Mountain Creek. The buffalo were gone. In order to have their dance, the Kiowas had to buy an animal from the domestic herd which Charles Goodnight preserved in Texas. In 1889 a Sun Dance was planned, but it was found out and prevented by the soldiers at Fort Sill. The Kiowas were going to suspend an old buffalo from the sacred tree. Perhaps the most immoral act ever committed against the land was the senseless killing of the buffalo.

The loss of the Sun Dance was the blow that killed the native Kiowa culture. The Kiowas might have endured every privation but that, the desecration of their faith. Without their religion there was nothing to sustain them. Subsequent acceptance of the Ghost Dance, peyote, and Christianity were for the Kiowas pathetic attempts to revive the old deities; they had become a people whose spirit was broken.

My grandmother lived in the old house where Cheyney came frequently to visit. It pleased her to dwell on the past, and her memory was keen. On the last day of a visit with her, she told me again of the red horse my grandfather trained to race. I have heard the story many times. The horse belonged to my great aunt, but my grandfather trained it, and it was his to race. When the Sun Dance was gone, the Kiowas came together to race their horses; it was their social time. The red horse was the swiftest runner in the territory. Again and again the Comanches and the Cheyennes and the Pawnees and the Caddoes matched their finest animals against it, but it always won. Half a century or less earlier, the red horse would have been anointed with the medicine of war—it would have been a hunter. When the red horse died, my grandfather placed its bones in a box and kept them in a barn. I can remember seeing them when I was a child. They were stolen some years ago.

It is appropriate to speak of the red horse. It is by no means coincidental that it should be in the foreground of my grandmother's memory. Nor is it remarkable that my grandfather should have preserved the bones of a horse—nor, for that matter, that they should have been thought valuable enough to steal. The horse is the factor which accounts for the fundamental difference between the legend of the man who found Tai-me and the tale of the Kiowa brothers. In the earlier setting, before there were horses, the storyteller is sharply aware of his own frailty; he is inhibited by the eternal prospects of pain, hunger, and despair. His mind is compelled to look beyond itself for ease; it recoils from the present world and fastens upon another. All this is turned quite around in the legend of the brothers. In the very motion of that story, there is a satisfaction in the here and now, an enthusiasm for the moment. This is not to imply that the reliance upon myth and religion has become less than integral; it is merely to observe that the storyteller has begun to find his world so various that it can fill and fascinate his whole mind.

About the time of the Pequod War, the Kiowa and the horse came simultaneously upon the southern plains. Then for a hundred years and more the Kiowa and the horse were one. The horse exerted a crucial influence upon virtually every aspect of Kiowa culture. It brought about a revolution.

From the pre-horse culture the Kiowas brought only a nomadism and a mythology; the horse brought a new and material way of life. The Kiowa pulled up the roots which had always held him to the ground. He was given the means to prevail against distance. For the first time he could move beyond the limits of his human strength, of his vision, even of his former dreams. No longer was it necessary to stalk the herds, to construct traps, and to carry the meat of the kill on foot. With the horse the Kiowa could acquire enough food in one day to last him many months. He could transport his possessions at will and with only a fraction of his former time and effort.

But the greatest change was psychological. Seated behind the withers of a horse, elevated to a height from which the far world was made a possession of the eye, sensually conscious of an immense fund of living power under him and nearly part of him, the Kiowa was greater than he was. When a Kiowa died, the throat of his hunting horse was cut over his grave. The horse bred in the Kiowa a certain defiance. It gave him a taste for danger and an inclination to belligerence. A predatory society is said to bear the seeds of its own destruction. Even at the high tide of the horse culture, when they were most warlike and most feared, the Kiowas could not defend all the quarters of their sway. They ranged over hundreds of miles in quest of quarrels and trophies. They resisted to the death every attempt on the part of the white man to take their land, even after all resistance was known to be futile.

When the principle of mobility by which they lived was stifled, when they were driven like cattle into the corrals at Fort Sill and their horses and weapons confiscated, the Kiowas degenerated. When the buffalo were gone and the Sun Dance was prohibited they suffered the loss of their last hope, hope itself. Degeneration is both the cause and effect of despair. The Kiowas had no immunity against the flood of alien forces which fell upon them in defeat. The white man's diseases ravaged them, his conveniences spoiled them, his liquor enslaved and corrupted them. They had returned to the ground actually and symbolically. The centaur was dead.

The sense of defeat is not easily overcome. As do all unrelieved conditions of life, it becomes in time personal and definitive—almost welcome, almost comfortable. In one respect the Pequods were spared the ultimate price of resistance, for they were made to surrender their lives only. The moral nature of the force which destroyed the Pequods and beggared the Kiowas had changed but little in two hundred years. Superficially, a witch-burning psychology had given way to an age of philanthropy. Substantially, however, the soldiers who turned from each other at the Wilderness and Gettysburg to oppose their common enemy on the frontier were moved by the same morality which had created violence elsewhere and before.

The morality of intolerance has become in the twentieth century a morality of pity. The American people might well be sensitive on the subject of Indian welfare. The very survival of the Indian race in its homeland has been an inglorious, not infrequently desperate, journal of abuse and shame. The contact with the white man's civilization—it was all too clear at the turn of the century—had failed entirely to enrich the Indian. To the contrary, that civilization had debased him. Surely the white man was hard put to retain his image of the noble savage. For what he saw in actuality—if he dared to look—was not the creature of his imagination but a poor, syphilitic, lice-infested wastrel whose only weapon against despair was alcohol. The death rate among Indians had begun to exceed the birth rate. The reservations had at last become contagious colonies and concentration camps.

The relaxation of intolerance and the rise of pity are significant foot-notes to the evolution of American morality. The Americanist Roy Harvey Pearce has written a unique book on the Indian and the idea of civilization. He observes quite accurately that pity and censure have suffused our understanding of the Indian: "The historical fact is that our civilization in subduing the Indian, killed its own creature, the savage. The living fact is that it has not yet been able entirely to kill the Indian, but having subdued him, no longer needs or cares to."

The federal government has compiled a poor record of preserving Indian lands. In 1849 the management of Indian affairs passed from the War Department to the Department of the Interior, an agency largely concerned with the task of dispersing public lands among private investors at nominal prices. In 1887, the year of the last Kiowa Sun Dance, Congress passed the Allotment Act, which provided for the subdivision of reservation land into individually owned parcels. With the changeover in federal management, and with the passage of the Allotment Act in particular, the white man began systematically to take possession of the reservations.

Allotment was an obvious and efficient means of land robbery. The mechanics of allotment were simple. The owner was required to hold possession of the land for a period of twenty-five years; then he was permitted to sell. If he should die, the allotment was to be divided equally among all his heirs. Quite arbitrarily the government determined the uniform size of allotments on a given reservation and distributed them among the enrolled members of the tribe. Frequently the total number of allotments comprised only a portion of the reservation. The "surplus" land was confiscated and opened to white settlement. The clause which required that land pass to all heirs in common resulted in a ludicrous, mathematical diminution of estates. Many allotments simply dissolved into worthless half acres in the midst of wastelands. In a two-year period following the inception of the allotment system, Indian lands were reduced by twenty million acres. By 1933 the tribes had been dispossessed of nearly one hundred million acres, and most of the remainder was under lease to whites.

The logic by which the government justified the Allotment Act was disarmingly sound in theory: tribal ownership of land was a deterrent to cultural assimilation; a sense of personal property—the pride of individual ownership—would lead directly to acculturation. But the theory failed. The allotments were too small to provide other than the barest agricultural sustenance. The Indians did not know how to farm, and no one saw fit to teach them. The Indians could only sell their land; only the whites could buy it. The land passed from Indian ownership seemingly by a process of natural law.

The politics of the New Deal ended allotment and improved the status of the Indian. Franklin D. Roosevelt appointed John Collier Commissioner of Indian Affairs. It was a fortunate choice. Collier was a social scientist. He recognized the importance of tribal identity to the psychological well-being of the Indian, and he acted upon his conviction that the Indian should remain on his own land, in an environment of his own making. He inaugurated educational programs for young and old alike, programs wholly related to the basic problem of survival: principles of husbandry, irrigation, home economy, soil conservation. The role of the reservation day school became paramount; it was a field laboratory in which the Indian might be exposed on his own terms and without urgency to the world around him. The Indian Service began to give preference to Indian job applicants, and major steps were taken to eradicate squalor and disease on the reservations.

The depression which generated and defined the New Deal inadvertently facilitated Collier's methods. Indian economic survival off the reservations was out of the question. The Civilian Conservation Corps sponsored an Indian division, which provided reservation employment for both whites and Indians. Infinitely more important, it provided an opportunity and an incentive for cooperation between the white man and the red on all levels of the intercultural relationship. Considerable progress was made toward the accomplishment of acculturation during the New Deal administration. It was an era of mutual discovery and respect—in all the best meeting ground that has yet been provided.

With the Second World War, and with the prosperity which followed, the national conscience shifted again with respect to the Indian. The morality of pity began to assume an attitude of impatience. The climate has become a curious hybrid of historical notions. On the surface it resembles that prejudice which stems directly from the assumption that the Indian is a passive and obstructive factor in the national life. On the other hand, it has been informed by the humanitarian temper of the nineteenth century.

The contemporary white American is willing to assume responsibility for the Indian—he is willing to take on the burdens of oppressed peoples everywhere—but he is decidedly unwilling to divest himself of the false assumptions which impede his good intentions. He is an ambiguous, even contradictory, man. He is rather like that historian of the Pequod War who reached for an analogy and got hold of a stereotype.

The Relocation Program was an attempt by the Bureau of Indian Affairs to accelerate integration. The program rewarded individual Indians who agreed to leave the reservations and take employment in the cities. The rewards of urban civilization, however, could not compensate for the loss of tribal identity, and more than 20 percent of the relocated Indians returned disenchanted to the reservations. Like allotment, relocation was attractive in theory. If an Indian consented to be relocated, his transportation expenses were paid by the government; he was provided with employment and lodging. He had access to recreational and counseling facilities, and he was entitled to the services of specially trained social workers.

The failure of relocation resided with the premise upon which it was based: that the Indian becomes a white man by virtue of living in the presence of white men. It is dangerous to assume that cultural assimilation can occur under ideal conditions over a period of many years; it is patently absurd to suppose that it might occur immediately in downtown Chicago or Los Angeles. The Indian in the city was victimized by the very things which define urban existence. He could neither understand nor be understood because his knowledge of English was inadequate; he could not support himself or his family because he knew nothing of urban economics; in particular he could not clear his mind of the innumerable doubts and fears which an alien civilization imposed upon him because he was an Indian. None but an Indian knows so well what it is like to have incomplete existence in two worlds and security in neither. Moreover, relocation was flagrantly misrepresented to the Indian. The accommodations he was given were commonly substandard. The ratio of social workers to relocated Indians was grossly inadequate. Indian alcoholism and delinquency were so prevalent as to be major problems in some metropolitan areas.

Relocation was especially interesting in a moral context. There were many who defended relocation for moral reasons. They deplored the idea of "putting the Indian away" on the reservation, of making him a second-class citizen. However righteous this indignation, it was misdirected. It is imperative to consider that the Indian is, for the time being, better off in his own world than in another. His is the only world in which he has a fighting chance. Certainly the Indian cannot remain indefinitely isolated; that is neither possible nor desirable. When the Indian no longer needs the reservation, he will leave it of his own accord.

The infamous Termination Bills, Congressional legislation designed to terminate federal responsibility for Indians at the earliest possible date, greatly retarded the process of acculturation. And these laws invited exploitation of Indian property. The Eisenhower administration, committed to a pledge of reduced federal power, initiated an all-out drive to place the states in charge of their Indian tribes. Long-established federal services such as Indian education and development of Indian land resources began suddenly to come under the jurisdiction and control of the state governments.

Indian education has been crucially affected by the cessation of federal management. State Departments of Education have made a strong bid to increase their rolls with Indian students for the reason that the federal government continues to allocate funds for the purpose of Indian education. For every Indian child enrolled in a public school, therefore, the national government has contributed to the coffers of public education. In consequence, there has been a strong temptation to place the emphasis upon profit rather than upon learning. Also, the infiltration of public schools by Indian students has resulted in a general retardation of the learning process. Because of the language differential and related factors the Indian child was well behind his white counterpart at every stage of formal education; moreover, the gap became wider at each successive stage. In an integrated classroom of white and Indian students, one or the other group has been neglected, and the learning potential of both has been unrealized.

In 1958–1959 I taught in a school in Dulce, New Mexico, which had recently been converted from a government Indian boarding school to a public day school. The student body was composed predominantly of Navajo and Apache youths; there was a small percentage of Anglo and Spanish students. Because the school was situated on a reservation, and because of its large number of Indian students, it was the wealthiest school in the entire district; its gleaming science laboratory was, as I remember, particularly impressive. Yet its public school curriculum was not in keeping with the needs of its particular student body. The Indian boys and girls who attended my classes were ill advised to study a foreign language before they had got possession of English or to pursue chemistry before they had learned how to grow sufficient food for their prospective families. They were bright young people, and their response was eager. Were they to be given the chance to apply their minds directly to their immediate world, rather than to a world that can only be for them hypothetical, they should soon repudiate that isolation which at once inhibits and sustains them.

Most public schools, of course, are off the reservations. The Indian children were forced to enter an environment in which their racial characteristics were made conspicuous and they themselves were made self-conscious. Public education at this time can only discourage that confidential relationship between teacher and pupil which is indispensable to the accomplishment of acculturation. The teacher needs, as fully as possible, to understand the way in which his students think. He needs to know as much about their world as he should like them to know about his, including its history, its language, and its beliefs. Such reciprocal learning is admittedly ideal rather than practical. Nevertheless, we should be always conscious of the ideal and come as close to it as we can.

"Where are you going?" That is the conventional formula of greeting at the eastern pueblo of Jemez, where I lived for almost twenty years. In 1946 the pueblo numbered about a thousand inhabitants. By the mid-sixties the population had grown by nearly 30 percent; the mode of transportation had changed from the horse and wagon to the automobile; electricity had replaced the old kerosene lamps and the flatirons and had introduced refrigeration; and a sewage system had been constructed. In order to appreciate fully the significance of these changes, one must, I suspect, have seen the world upon which they were wrought. The forces of civilization and progress have moved across the pueblo like a glacier and, in their path, nothing can ever be the same again.

Convenience has brought the old attendant ills. Alcoholism has become a menace of frightening proportions. Juvenile delinquency, unknown to Jemez in 1946, has been a cancerous problem since the 1960s. A number of Jemez tribesmen migrated to the cities under the auspices of relocation, and a number returned to sit in gloom and lethargy. Jemez is in a sense a late chapter in the history of Indian-white confrontation. In adherence to the general pattern of which I spoke earlier, the age-old cultural conflict now centers upon the sedentary reservations of the southwestern United States.

The pueblos are the most anachronistic clusters of humanity in this country. In spite of the influence which the modern world has exerted upon them, they remain islands of refuge in time and space, committed absolutely to the principles of independence and isolation. For three hundred years the pueblos remained nearly impervious to the white man's interference, but after the Second World War, and with the adoption of such concepts as relocation and termination in particular, the old ways were lost. The sense of temporality which has pervaded the old *costumbres* is, one thinks, an illusion produced by the sad certainty that, beyond these sanctuaries, cultural extinction is imminent.

There is in Indian towns also a sense of timelessness and peace. No one who has watched the winter solstice ceremonies at Jemez can have failed to perceive the great spiritual harmonies which culminate in those ancient rites. None who has heard the deep droning concert of the singers and the insistent vibration of the drums can have mistaken the old, sacred respect for sound and silence which makes the magic of words and literatures.

More symbolic of the cultural spirit even than these is the race which is run at dawn before the spring clearing of the Jemez irrigation ditches. The course is south of the town, on the old wagon road which runs to San Ysidro. It is a stickball race; the runners imitate the Cloud people who fill the arroyos with life-giving rain, and keep in motion, with only their feet, a stickball which represents the moving drift at the water's edge. The first race each year comes in February, when the dawn is clear and cold, and the runners breathe steam. It is a long race, and it is neither won nor lost. It is an expression of the soul in the ancient terms of sheer physical exertion. To watch those runners is to know that they draw with every step some elemental power which resides at the core of the earth and which, for all our civilized ways, is lost upon us who have lost the art of going with the flow of things. In the tempo of that race there is time to ponder morality and demoralization, hungry wolves and falling stars. And there is time to puzzle over that curious and fortuitous question with which the people of Jemez greet each other. It is a question we might put in our own mouths to ward off the immorality of indifference.

* * *

AFTERWORD

"The Morality of Indian Hating" is the earliest of the essays in this collection, written when I was a student at Stanford in 1962 or 1963, as I recall. It is political in character, and its focus is on a time in the past. In the late 1990s, it seems a kind of anachronism. In certain aspects it reflects a world that has changed remarkably in the last thirty years. The essay is no longer timely in all of its parts.

Nothwithstanding, the essential statement of the essay—that the American Indian is, and has been from the moment of contact, engaged in a desperate struggle to persist in his cultural and spiritual being—is at least as true now as it was when I wrote it.

Moreover, as seen in the context of the collection as a whole, "The Morality of Indian Hating" may be a considerable moment in the evolution of the man made of words.

My convictions have grown stronger. I believe that what most threatens the American Indian is sacrilege, the theft of the sacred. Inexorably the Indian people have been, and are being, deprived of the spiritual nourishment that has sustained them for many thousands of years. This is a subtle holocaust, and it is ongoing. It is imperative that the Indian defines himself, that he finds the strength to do so, that he refuses to let others define him. Children are at greatest risk. We, Native Americans in particular, but all of us, need to restore the sacred to our children. It is a matter of the greatest importance.

The Centaur Complex

Like Alexander of Macedon, I was given a horse when I was twelve years old. I calculate that I rode several thousands of miles on my horse in the following four or five years. After a time the horse became the extension of my senses, touching me to the earth, the air, and the sun more perfectly than I could touch these things for myself. Separate creatures though we were, there were moments when there was practically no telling us apart. We were one whole and distinct image in the plane—indeed more than an image, an entity of substance.

The centaur is surely one of man's more ennobling and perdurable representations of himself, for, like Pan and the angels, it seems at once to comprehend and exceed the human condition. And popularly, at least, it is a masculine one. I cannot recall ever having seen the depiction of a centaur in which the human half was apparently female. Such depictions, if they exist, are no doubt rare, as indeed are likenesses of the mounted Saint Joan, Lady Godiva, and even those numerous frames from *National Velvet*, as compared to the hordes of manly Cossacks, Magyars, chargers of the Light Brigade, cowboys and Indians that pervade all illustrated histories of the world.

When Alexander was twelve his father, Philip, gave him the black horse Bucephalus. Historians tell us that the horse was purchased from a Thessalian breeder. (The race of centaurs dwelt in the mountains of Thessaly). Alexander kept the beloved animal at his hand for twenty years, leading it gently, when it was too old to ride, in his campaigns, so that the scent of conquest and glory should lie in its nostrils to the end of its days. There is no legend of Alexander without Bucephalus.

Men and horses have performed great feats together. Probably the greatest single feat has gone unrecorded, and that is as it should be. It happened one day long ago, it may be, on the steppes of Central Asia, or perhaps on an early morning on the misty grasses of the Great Plains.

Some remarkable things have been recorded. William Frederick Cody, "Buffalo Bill," scout, Indian fighter, buffalo hunter extraordinaire, was something of a centaur. He was a Pony Express rider at the age of fourteen. Once he rode, without relief, a distance of 320 miles. As a scout for the 5th Cavalry he is reported by his commander, General Philip Sheridan, to have ridden 350 miles on horseback in less than sixty hours. Beyond the dubious distinction that Buffalo Bill killed more American bisons than any other man, and beyond the great ballyhoo of the Wild West Show, which eventually caught Cody up and devoured him, is the fact that he was a horseman of nearly incredible accomplishment. The little boy in me wants to see Cody setting out, at first light, on a day's work. There is inspiration in that.

My own favorite story of the centaur is one in which the human element is all too human, from the Kiowa:

> There was a man who owned a fine hunting horse. The horse was black and fast and afraid of nothing. When it was turned upon an enemy it struck at full speed. The man need have no hand upon the rein. But, you know, that man knew fear. Once, during a charge, he turned that animal from its course. That was a bad thing. The hunting horse died of shame.

But in our own time, consider: the man and the horse are one. They make one image in the busy, brightly colored field. The expectation is that of one, preeminent flash of color on the finish line. The great horse Secretariat and his jockey Ron Turcotte are the brilliant creature, the centaur in view. It is a bright, warm day in June, 1973, at Belmont Park. The centaur, in blue and white blocks, prances out, calm and collected. There is no waste, no nervousness, no hint of panic. It is the first into the starting gate.

Seventy thousand people are looking on. They are about to see the greatest performance by a racehorse in the twentieth century. The Triple

Crown has been won eight times before, most recently by Citation in 1948. Secretariat breaks clean on the inside. Sham, too, breaks clean. Sham has lost to Secretariat in both the Kentucky Derby and the Preakness by two and a half lengths in each race. He is primed to challenge at this longer distance. Secretariat runs the quarter in 23 and three fifths, the half in 46 and one fifth, the six furlongs in 1:09 and four fifths, the mile in 1:34 and one fifth, the mile and a quarter in 1:59. And, to the astonishment of everyone there, he just keeps extending his lead—7, 10, 12, 14 lengths. Turning for home after a mile and a quarter he is 20 lengths in front. Sham, his heart broken, has faded to last place. At the eighth pole Secretariat is 28 lengths ahead of Twice a Prince, the Place horse. He wins by 31 lengths, at a final time of 2:24, the fastest mile and a half ever run on a dirt track.

The time was not important. The deed was. For a moment, on that day in early summer, over two decades ago, we were privileged to see greatness undiluted, greatness as it is in the flesh, even without advertisement or fanfare.

A Divine Blindness: The Place of Words in a State of Grace

The great Argentine writer Jorge Luis Borges loved words and books, and he lived his life in the immediate presence of words and books. Indeed, his life, and the element of language in which he lived, were indivisible. We cannot imagine his existence along us, a man made of flesh and blood, a man who walked in the sunlit streets of Buenos Aires, chatted with friends, and ate good food and drank good wine, who slept and dreamed in the light of the moon, unless we imagine as well the language in which he placed these things. And we must remember that he was blind. That makes a difference. He gave us to understand that our human experience, however intense it may be, is truly valid only in proportion as it is expressed in words. "Expression" is a word and a concept that he loved. Poetry, he believed, is expression, and it is founded upon an aesthetic. In our time and place we are distracted by the notion of "communication," which is perhaps inferior to expression. I believe that Borges thought so.

Borges was a blind man. And yet he could see farther into the world than most sighted people. Much farther. He was named director of the National Library of Argentina. And in a famous lecture he wrote:

> Little by little I came to realize the strange irony of events. I had always imagined Paradise as a kind of library. Others think of a garden or of a palace. There I was, the center, in a way, of nine hundred thousand books in various languages, but I found I could barely make out the title pages and the spines. I wrote the "Poem of the Gifts," which begins:

No one should read self-pity or reproach
into this statement of the majesty
of God; who with such splendid irony
granted me books and blindness at one touch.

Imagine! Blindness and books! Here is an equation that seems hopeless. And yet Borges made of it the cornerstone and definition of his being. So did the blind Homer, perhaps, make as much of a balance between oral tradition and the history of the Trojan wars.

Oral tradition is the other side of the miracle of language. As important as books are—as important as writing is, there is yet another, a fourth dimension of language which is just as important, and which, indeed, is older and more nearly universal than writing: the oral tradition, that is, the telling of stories, the recitation of epic poems, the singing of songs, the making of prayers, the chanting of magic and mystery, the exertion of the human voice upon the unknown—in short, the spoken word. In the history of the world nothing has been more powerful than that ancient and irresistible tradition of *vox humana*. That tradition is especially and above all the seat of the imagination, and the imagination is a kind of divine blindness in which we see not with our eyes but with our minds and souls, in which we dream the world and our being in it. It is no wonder that Borges found all color and brilliance in words and languages.

When the subtitle "The Place of Words in a State of Grace" occurred to me, in the back of my mind was this poem by Emily Dickinson:

Further in Summer than the Birds
Pathetic from the Grass
A minor Nation celebrates
Its unobtrusive Mass.

No Ordinance be seen
So gradual the Grace
A pensive Custom it becomes
Enlarging Loneliness.

Antiquest felt at Noon
When August burning low
Arise this spectral Canticle
Repose to typify

Remit as yet no Grace
No Furrow on the Glow
Yet a Druidic Difference
Enhances Nature now

This poem, written about 1866 by a then obscure woman poet in the Connecticut Valley of western Massachusetts, is one of the great moments in American literature. The statement of the poem is profound; it remarks the absolute separation between man and nature at a precise moment in time. The poet looks as far as she can into the natural world, but what she sees at last is her isolation from that world. She perceives, that is, the limits of her own perception. But that, we reason, is enough. This poem of just more than sixty words comprehends the human condition in relation to the universe:

So gradual the Grace
A pensive Custom it becomes
Enlarging Loneliness.

But this is a divine loneliness, the loneliness of a species evolved far beyond all others. The poem bespeaks a state of grace. In its precision, perception, and eloquence it establishes the place of words within that state. Words are indivisible with the highest realization of human being.

It happens that one of my chief interests is the oral tradition, language as it is spoken rather than written. But it is appropriate to consider writing, as well. We spend our lives, if we are fortunate, in the presence of books. Books are to be read; they are to be consumed and digested; they are to be turned over in the mind; they are to be taken seriously. It may be that these principles are threatened in our time—as they have always been threatened, I suppose. I heard recently of a little boy who, when asked where his mother was, replied, "She's in the den, watching a book."

The late Loren Eiseley wrote:

> Man without writing cannot long retain his history in his head. His intelligence permits him to grasp some kind of succession of generations; but without writing, the tale of the past rapidly degenerates into fumbling myth and fable. Man's greatest epic, his four long battles with the advancing ice of the great continental glaciers, has vanished from human memory without a trace. Our illiterate fathers disappeared and with them, in a few scant generations, died one of the great stories of all time. This episode has nothing to do with the biological quality of a brain as between then and now. It has to do instead with a device, an invention made possible by the hand. That invention came too late in time to record eyewitness accounts of the years of the Giant Frost.

The book is a wonderful invention. Emily Dickinson's poem tells us that we have our best existence within the element of language. And the book is a concentration of that element, a whole realization of our experience in the world of ideas, and, as such, it is a thing of infinite possibility. What in the world is there that cannot, in some viable way, be contained within the pages of a book?

In one of his most provocative stories Jorge Luis Borges writes of the Aleph, which is, he says, a point in space in which all other points in space are contained. This idea—which is an idea of the infinite—might almost stand as a definition of the book. There is, by the way, a fascinating correlation here. The Aleph, as you know, is the first letter of the Hebrew alphabet and is therefore in a literal sense the character—the point, if you will—in which alphabetic writing and the book as we know it have their origin.

It is now generally accepted that the alphabet was invented about 1800 B.C. within the complex that is known as the Northwest Semitic

Linguistic Group, which includes the Canaanites, the Hebrews, the Phoenicians, and the Aramaeans. Moreover, it appears that the alphabet is indeed original and originative, that it was invented once, and that all alphabetic writing is derived from that one invention. That alphabetic writing passed successively from the Semitics to the Greeks to the Etruscans to the Romans to our own civilization suggests a continuity in intellectual history that is surely one of the greatest achievements of man. Every book, in one way or another, perpetuates that achievement and celebrates it.

Writing is about six thousand years old, as far as we know, not a long time in the tenure of man upon this planet. And the book as we know it—the printed book—is an altogether modern phenomenon in terms of that scale. The first extant printed book is the *Dharani Sutra*, printed from woodblocks between A.D. 704 and 751. It is a twenty-foot-long Chinese scroll (the text is a Buddhist scripture), found in a Korean monastery in 1966.

The first dated printed book known to us is the *Diamond Sutra*, also printed from woodblocks, found in China in the Caves of the Thousand Buddhas. It bears the date A.D. May 11, 868.

The first extant book printed from movable type is the 42-line Bible, usually attributed to Johann Gutenberg, printed between 1452 and 1456 in Mainz. The first dated book produced from movable type is the 1457 Psalter, printed by Foust and Schoeffer in Mainz.

The book in America is even more recent, of course. The Reverend Jose Glover purchased a printing press in his native England and carried it with him when he embarked for Massachusetts in the summer of 1638. He died en route, but his press came into New England in the possession of his widow. This first English-American press was set up at Cambridge, the seat of Harvard College, late in 1638. In 1640 *The Whole Booke of Psalms* (or the "Bay Psalm Book," as it is more commonly known), edited by Richard Mather, came from this press as a volume in quarto of 148 leaves. In 1663 there was issued from this same press John Eliot's translation of the whole Bible into the Algonquin tongue.

But in America there is something else, a continuum of language that goes back thousands of years before the printing press—back to the times of origin—an indigenous expression, an utterance that proceeds from the very intelligence of the soil: the oral tradition.

Alastair Reid tells us that Borges was not especially concerned with literary criticism. "For him," Reid writes, "literature at its highest point generates awe, the disquieting astonishment that arises from a poem, a deep image, a crucial paragraph, what he calls either *asombro* or *sagrada horror*, 'holy dread.' "

The *asombro*, the *sagrada horror*, this awe and disquieting astonishment, is at the heart of the oral tradition, as Borges well knew. And it arises from a song, indeed a deep image, a crucial prayer, the central character of the human voice itself. What Borges most esteemed in writing, in those great books he knew but could not see to read, I suspect, were precisely the things that distinguish the oral tradition—awe, astonishment, imagination, belief, holy dread.

I would like to have heard the voices of those ancients who crossed the Bering Bridge to the North American continent thirty thousand years ago. They would be unintelligible to me, I'm sure, meaningless except at the level of the imagination, which is the great matrix of oral tradition. Certainly there were storytellers among them, singers, makers of prayers, what we call poets.

> *In the north*
> *the wind*
> *blows*
> *they are walking*
> *the hail*
> *beats*
> *they are walking*

This song from the Sioux Buffalo Dance, or something very close to it, might well have been sung by hunters coming across the Bering Bridge in pursuit of those great beasts which roamed the paleolithic north, the corridor from Beringia to the Great Plains of the North American continent.

I wrote a poem entitled "At Risk," which bears some relation to this ancient song, I believe:

> *I played at words.*
> *It was a long season.*
>
> *Soft syllables,*
> *Images that shimmered,*
> *Intricate etymologies.*
>
> *They cohered in wonder.*
> *I was enchanted.*
>
> *My soul was at risk.*
> *I struggled*
> *Towards hurt,*
> *Towards healing,*
> *Towards passion,*
> *Towards peace.*
>
> *I wheeled in the shadow of a hawk.*
> *Dizziness came upon me;*
> *The turns of time confined and confounded me.*
>
> *I lay in a cave,*
> *On a floor cured in blood.*
>
> *Ancient animals danced about me,*
> *Presenting themselves formally,*
> *In masks.*
>
> *And there was I, among ancient animals,*
> *In the formality of the dance,*
> *Remembering my face in the mirror of masks.*

The distance between these two songs is very great in time. If you imagine, as I do, that the Buffalo Dance song was sung not only by the Lakota buffalo hunters of the nineteenth century, but by the so-called

Paleo Indians of the last Ice Age, we are talking not about generations but about millennia. We are talking about the life and the life span of words. We are talking about the deepest sustenance of the human race. We are talking; we are *talking*. If words are the intricate bonds of language, and if the spoken word is the first part of this ancient design, this construction that makes of us a family, a tribe, a civilization, we had better strive to understand how and why—and perhaps first of all, *that*—we exist in the element of language.

Language is the context of our experience. We know who we have been, who we are, and who we can be in the dimension of words, of language. Here is my own song:

> *I am a feather in the bright sky*
> *I am the blue horse that runs in the plain*
> *I am the fish that rolls, shining, in the water*
> *I am the shadow that follows a child*
> *I am the evening light, the lustre of meadows*
> *I am an eagle playing with the wind*
> *I am a cluster of bright beads*
> *I am the farthest star*
> *I am the cold of the dawn*
> *I am the roaring of the rain*
> *I am the glitter on the crust of the snow*
> *I am the long track of the moon in a lake*
> *I am a flame of four colors*
> *I am a deer standing away in the dusk*
> *I am a field of sumac and the pomme blanche*
> *I am an angle of geese in the winter sky*
> *I am the hunger of a young wolf*
> *I am the whole dream of these things*
>
> *You see, I am alive, I am alive*
> *I stand in good relation to the earth*
> *I stand in good relation to the gods*
> *I stand in good relation to all that is beautiful*

I stand in good relation to the daughter of Tsen-tainte
You see, I am alive, I am alive

This is to say that Paradise is a library. It is also a prairie and a plain, and it is a place of the imagination, the place of words in a state of grace. In the mind's eye we can see into it more perfectly than we otherwise can. It is the miracle of language that enables us to do so.

The American West and the Burden of Belief

I

West of Jemez Pueblo there is a great red mesa, and in the folds of the earth at its base there is a canyon, the dark red walls of which are sheer and shadow stained; they rise vertically to a remarkable height. You do not suspect that the canyon is there, but you turn a corner and the walls contain you; you look into a corridor of geologic time. When I went into that place I left my horse outside, for there was a strange light and quiet upon the walls, and the shadows closed upon me. I looked up, straight up, to the serpentine strip of the sky. It was clear and deep, like a river running across the top of the world. The sand in which I stood was deep, and I could feel the cold of it through the soles of my shoes. And when I walked out, the light and heat of the day struck me so hard that I nearly fell. On the side of a hill in the plain of the Hissar I saw my horse grazing among sheep. The land inclined into the distance, to the Pamirs, to the Fedchenko Glacier. The river which I had seen near the sun had run out into the endless ether above the Karakoram range and the Plateau of Tibet.

When I wrote this passage in *The Names*, some years ago, it did not seem strange to me that two such landscapes as that of northern New Mexico and that of Central Asia should become one in the mind's eye and in the confluence of image and imagination. Nor does it seem strange to me now. Even as we look back, the partitions of our experience open and close upon each other; disparate realities coalesce into a single, integrated appearance.

This transformation is perhaps the essence of art and literature. Certainly it is the soul of drama, and historically it is how we have seen the American West. Our human tendency is to concentrate the world upon a stage. We construct proscenium arches and frames in order to contain the thing that is larger than our comprehension, the plane of boundless possibility, that which reaches almost beyond wonder. Sometimes the process of concentration results in something like a burden of belief, a kind of ambiguous exaggeration, as in the paintings of Albert Bierstadt, say, or in the photographs of Ansel Adams, in which an artful grandeur seems superimposed upon a grandeur that is innate. Or music comes to mind, a music that seems to pervade the vast landscape and emanate from it, not the music of wind and rain and birds and beasts, but Virgil Thomson's *The Plow that Broke the Plains*, or Aaron Copland's *Rodeo*, or perhaps the soundtrack from *The Alamo* or *She Wore a Yellow Ribbon*. We are speaking of overlays, impositions, a kind of narcissism that locates us within our own field of vision. But if this is a distorted view of the West, it is nonetheless a view that fascinates us.

And more often than not the fascination consists in peril. In *My Life on the Plains*, George Armstrong Custer describes a strange sight:

> I have seen a train of government wagons with white canvas covers moving through a mirage which, by elevating the wagons to treble their height and magnifying the size of the covers, presented the appearance of a line of large sailing vessels under full sail, while the usual appearance of the mirage gave a correct likeness of an immense lake or sea. Sometimes the mirage has been the cause of frightful suffering and death by its deceptive appearance.

He goes on to tell of emigrants to California and Oregon who, suffering terrible thirst, were deflected from their route by a mirage, "like an *ignis fatuus*," and so perished. Their graves are strewn far and wide over the prairie.

This equation of wonder and peril is for Custer a kind of exhilaration, as indeed it is for most of those adventurers who journeyed westward, and even for those who did not, who escaped into the Wild West Show or the dime novel.

For the European who came from a community of congestion and confinement, the West was beyond dreaming; it must have inspired him to formulate an idea of the infinite. There he could walk through geologic time; he could see into eternity. He was surely bewildered, wary, afraid. The landscape was anomalously beautiful and hostile. It was desolate and unforgiving, and yet it was a world of paradisal possibility. Above all, it was wild, definitively wild. And it was inhabited by people who were to him altogether alien and inscrutable, who were essentially dangerous and deceptive, often invisible, who were savage and unholy— and who were perfectly at home.

This is a crucial point, then: the West was occupied. It was the home of peoples who had come upon the North American continent many thousands of years before, who had in the course of their habitation become the spirit and intelligence of the earth, who had died into the ground again and again and so made it sacred. Those Europeans who ventured into the West must have seen themselves in some way as latecomers and intruders. In spite of their narcissism, some aspect of their intrusion must have occurred to them as sacrilege, for they were in the unfortunate position of robbing the native peoples of their homeland and the land of its spiritual resources. By virtue of their culture and history—a culture of acquisition and a history of conquest—they were peculiarly prepared to commit sacrilege, the theft of the sacred.

Even the Indians succumbed to the kind of narcissism the Europeans brought to bear on the primeval landscape, the imposition of a belief— essentially alien to both the land and the peoples who inhabited it— that would locate them once again within their own field of vision. For the Indian, the mirage of the Ghost Dance—to which the concepts of a messiah and immortality, both foreign, European imports, were central—was surely an *ignis fatuus*, and the cause of frightful suffering and death.

II

George Armstrong Custer had an eye to the country of the Great Plains, and especially to those of its features which constituted a "deceptive appearance." In November 1868, as he stealthily approached Black Kettle's camp on the Washita River, where he was to win his principal acclaim as an Indian fighter, he and his men caught sight of a strange thing. At the first sign of dawn there appeared a bright light ascending slowly from the skyline. Custer describes it sharply, even eloquently:

> Slowly and majestically it continued to rise above the crest of the hill, first appearing as a small brilliant flaming globe of bright golden hue. As it ascended still higher it seemed to increase in size, to move more slowly, while its colors rapidly changed from one to the other, exhibiting in turn the most beautiful combinations of prismatic tints.

Custer and his men took it to be a rocket, some sort of signal, and they assumed that their presence had been detected by the Indians. Here again is the equation of fascination and peril. But at last the reality is discovered:

> Rising above the mystifying influences of the atmosphere, that which had appeared so suddenly before us and excited our greatest apprehensions developed into the brightest and most beautiful of morning stars.

In the ensuing raid upon Black Kettle's camp, Custer and his troopers, charging to the strains of "Garry Owen," killed 103 Cheyennes, including Black Kettle and his wife. Ninety-two of the slain Cheyennes were women, children, and old men. Fifty-three women and children were captured. Custer's casualties totaled one officer killed, one officer severely and two more slightly wounded, and eleven troopers wounded. After the fighting, Custer ordered the herd of Indian ponies slain; the herd numbered 875 animals. "We did not need the ponies, while the Indians did," he wrote.

In the matter of killing women and children, Custer's exculpatory rhetoric seems lame, far beneath his poetic descriptions of mirages and the break of day:

> Before engaging in the fight orders had been given to prevent
> the killing of any but the fighting strength of the village; but in
> a struggle of this character it is impossible at all times to dis-
> criminate, particularly when, in a hand-to-hand conflict such as
> the one the troops were then engaged in, the squaws are as
> dangerous adversaries as the warriors, while Indian boys between
> ten and fifteen years of age were found as expert and determined
> in the use of the pistol and bow and arrow as the older warriors.

After the fighting, Black Kettle's sister, Mah-wis-sa, implored Custer to leave the Cheyennes in peace. Custer reports that she approached him with a young woman, perhaps seventeen years old, and placed the girl's hand in his. Then she proceeded to speak solemnly in her own language, words which Custer took to be a kind of benediction, with appropriate manners and gestures. When the formalities seemed to come to a close, Mah-wis-sa looked reverently to the skies and at the same time drew her hands slowly down over the faces of Custer and the girl. At this point Custer was moved to ask Romeo, his interpreter, what was going on. Romeo replied that Custer and the young woman had just been married to each other.

It is said that Mah-wis-sa told Custer that if he ever again made war on the Cheyennes, he would die. When he was killed at the Little Bighorn, Cheyenne women pierced his eardrums with awls, so that he might hear in the afterlife; he had failed to hear the warning given him at the Washita.

In the final paragraph of *My Life on the Plains*, Custer bids farewell to his readers and announces his intention "to visit a region of country as yet unseen by human eyes, except those of the Indian—a country described by the latter as abounding in game of all varieties, rich in scientific interest, and of surpassing beauty in natural scenery." After rumors of gold had made the Black Hills a name known throughout the country, General (then Lieutenant Colonel) George Armstrong Custer led an expedition from Fort Abraham Lincoln into the Black Hills in July and August, 1874. The Custer expedition traveled six hundred miles in sixty days. Custer reported proof of gold, but he had an eye to other things as well. He wrote in his diary:

> Every step of our march that day was amid flowers of the most exquisite colors and perfume. So luxuriant in growth were they that men plucked them without dismounting from the saddle . . . It was a strange sight to glance back at the advancing columns of cavalry and behold the men with beautiful bouquets in their hands, while the headgear of the horses was decorated with wreaths of flowers fit to crown a queen of May. Deeming it a most fitting appellation, I named this Floral Valley.

In the evening of that same day, sitting at mess in a meadow, the officers competed to see how many different flowers could be picked by each man, without leaving his seat. Seven varieties were gathered so. Some fifty different flowers were blooming in Floral Valley.

Imagine that Custer dreamed that night. In his dream he saw a man approaching on horseback, approaching slowly across a meadow full of wildflowers. The man drew very close and stopped, sitting straight up on the horse, holding Custer fast in his gaze. There could be no doubt that he was a warrior, and fearless, though he flourished no scalps and made no signs of fighting. His unbound hair hung below his waist. His body was painted with hail spots, a white bolt of lightning ran down one of his cheeks, and on his head he wore the feathers of a red-backed hawk. Except for moccasins and breechcloth he was naked.

> "I am George Armstrong Custer," Custer said, "called Yellow-hair, called Son of the Morning Star."
> "I am Curly," the man said, "called Crazy Horse."

And Custer wept for the nobility and dignity and greatness of the man facing him. And through his tears he perceived the brilliance of the meadow. The wildflowers were innumerable and more beautiful than anything he had ever seen or imagined. And when he thought his heart could bear no more, a thousand butterflies rose up, glancing and darting and floating around him, to spangle the sky, to become prisms of the sun. And he awoke serene and refreshed in his soul.

George Armstrong Custer sees the light upon the meadows of the plains, but he does not see disaster lurking at the Little Bighorn. He hears the bugles and the band, but he does not hear or heed the warning of the Cheyenne women. All about there is deception; the West is other than it seems.

III

In 1872, William Frederick Cody was awarded the Medal of Honor for his valor in fighting Indians. In 1913, army regulations specified that only enlisted men and officers were eligible to receive the Medal of Honor, and Cody's medal was therefore withdrawn and his name removed from the records. In 1916, after deliberation, the army decided to return the medal, having declared that Cody's service to his country was "above and beyond the call of duty."

Ambivalence and ambiguity, like deception, bear upon all definitions of the American West. The real issue of Cody's skill and accomplishment as an Indian fighter is not brought into question in this matter of the Medal of Honor, but it might be. Beyond the countless Indians he "killed" in the arena of the Wild West Show, Cody's achievements as an Indian fighter are suspect. Indeed, much of Cody's life is clouded in ambiguity. He claimed that in 1859 he became a Pony Express rider, but the Pony Express did not come into being until 1860. Even the sobriquet "Buffalo Bill" belonged to William Mathewson before it belonged to William Frederick Cody.

Buffalo Bill Cody was an icon and an enigma, and he was in some sense his own invention. One of his biographers wrote that he was "a man who was so much more than a western myth." One must doubt it, for the mythic dimension of the American West is an equation much greater than the sum of its parts. It would be more accurate, in this case, to say that the one dissolved into the other, that the man and myth became indivisible. The great fascination and peril of Cody's life was the riddle of who he was. The thing that opposed him, and perhaps betrayed him, was above all else the mirage of his own identity.

If we are to understand the central irony of Buffalo Bill and the Wild West Show, we must first understand that William Frederick Cody was an authentic western hero. As a scout, a guide, a marksman, and a buffalo hunter, he was second to none. At a time when horsemanship was at its highest level in America, he was a horseman nearly without peer. He defined the Plainsman. The authority of his life on the plains far surpassed Custer's.

But let us imagine that we are at Omaha, Nebraska, on May 17, 1883, in a crowd of eight thousand people. The spectacle of the "Wild West" unfolds before us. The opening parade is led by a twenty-piece band playing "Garry Owen," perhaps, or "The Girl I Left Behind Me." Then there comes an Indian in full regalia on a paint pony. Next are buffalo, three adults and a calf. Then there is Buffalo Bill, mounted on a fine white horse and resplendent in a great white hat, a fringed buckskin coat, and glossy thigh boots. He stands out in a procession of cowboys, Indians, more buffalo, and the Deadwood Stage, drawn by six handsome mules; the end is brought up by another band, playing "Annie Laurie" or "When Johnny Comes Marching Home." Then we see the acts—the racing of the Pony Express, exhibitions of shooting, the attack on the Deadwood Stage, and the finale of the great buffalo chase. Buffalo Bill makes a stirring speech, and we are enthralled; the applause is thunderous. But this is only a modest beginning, a mere glimpse of things to come.

What we have in this explosion of color and fanfare is an epic transformation of the American West into a traveling circus and of an American hero into an imitation of himself. Here is a theme with which we have become more than familiar. We have seen the transformation take place numberless times on the stage, on television and movie screens, and on the pages of comic books, dime novels and literary masterpieces. One function of the American imagination is to reduce the American landscape to size, to fit that great expanse to the confinement of the emigrant mind. It is a way to persist in our cultural being. We photograph ourselves on the rim of Monument Valley or against the wall of the Tetons, and we become our own frame of reference. As long as we can transform the landscape to accommodate our fragile presence, we can be saved. As long as we can see ourselves on the picture plane, we cannot be lost.

Arthur Kopit's play *Indians* is a remarkable treatise on this very subject of transformation. It can and ought to be seen as a tragedy, for its central story is that of Buffalo Bill's fatal passage into myth. He is constrained to translate his real heroism into a false and concentrated reflection of itself. The presence of the Indians is pervasive, but he cannot see them until they are called to his attention.

> BUFFALO BILL: THANK YOU, THANK YOU! A GREAT show lined up tonight! With all-time favorite Johnny Baker, Texas Jack and his twelve-string guitar, the Dancin' Cavanaughs, Sheriff Brad and the Deadwood Mail Coach, Harry Philamee's Trained Prairie Dogs, the Abilene County Girl's Trick Roping and Lasso Society, Pecos Pete and the—
>
> VOICE: *Bill.*
> BUFFALO BILL (*startled*): Hm?
> VOICE: Bring on the Indians.
> BUFFALO BILL: What?
> VOICE: The *Indians.*
> BUFFALO BILL: Ah...

Solemnly the Indians appear. In effect they shame Buffalo Bill; they tread upon his conscience. They fascinate and imperil him. By degrees his desperation to justify himself—and by extension the white man's treatment of the Indians in general—grows and becomes a burden too great to bear. In the end he sits trembling while the stage goes completely black. Then all lights up, rodeo music, the glaring and blaring; enter the Roughriders of the World! Buffalo Bill enters on his white stallion and tours the ring, doffing his hat to the invisible crowd. The Roughriders exit, and the Indians approach, and the lights fade to black again.

At five minutes past noon on January 10, 1917, Buffalo Bill died. Western Union ordered all lines cleared, and, in a state of war, the world was given the news at once. The old scout had passed on. Tributes and condolences came from every quarter, from children, from old soldiers, from heads of state.

In ambivalence and ambiguity, Cody died as he had lived. A week before his death, it was reported that Buffalo Bill had been baptized into the Roman Catholic Church. His wife Louisa was, however, said to be an Episcopalian, and his sister Julia, to whom he declared, "Your church suits me," was a Presbyterian. Following his death there was a controversy as to where Cody should be buried. He had often expressed the wish to be buried on Cedar Mountain, Wyoming. Nonetheless, his final resting place is atop Mount Lookout, above Denver, Colorado, overlooking the urban sprawl.

IV

DECEMBER 29, 1890
Wounded Knee Creek

In the shine of photographs
are the slain, frozen and black

on a simple field of snow.
They image ceremony:

women and children dancing,
old men prancing, making fun.

In autumn there were songs, long
since muted in the blizzard.

In summer the wild buckwheat
shone like fox fur and quillwork,

and dusk guttered on the creek.
Now in serene attitudes

of dance, the dead in glossy
death are drawn in ancient light.

On December 15, 1890, the great Hunkpapa leader, Sitting Bull, who had opposed Custer at the Little Bighorn and who had toured for a time with Buffalo Bill and the Wild West Show, was killed on the Standing Rock Reservation. In a dream he had foreseen his death at the hands of his own people.

Just two weeks later, on the morning of December 29, 1890, on Wounded Knee Creek near the Pine Ridge Agency, the 7th Cavalry of the United States Army opened fire on an encampment of Big Foot's band of Miniconjou Sioux. When the shooting ended, Big Foot and most of his people were dead or dying. It has been estimated that nearly three hundred of the original 350 men, women, and children in the camp were slain. Twenty-five soldiers were killed and thirty-nine wounded, most of them caught in their own fire.

Sitting Bull is reported to have said, "I am the last Indian." In some sense he was right. During his lifetime the world of the Plains Indians had changed forever. The old roving life of the buffalo hunters was over. A terrible disintegration, demoralization, had set in. If the death of Sitting Bull marked the end of an age, Wounded Knee marked the end of a culture.

I did not know then how much was ended. When I look back now from the high hill of my old age, I can still see the butchered women and children lying heaped and scattered all along the crooked gulch as plain as when I saw them with eyes still young. And I can see that something else died there in the bloody mud, and was buried in the blizzard. A people's dream died there. It was a beautiful dream.   —Black Elk

In the following days there were further developments. On January 7, 1891, nine days after the massacre at Wounded Knee, a young Sioux warrior named Plenty Horses shot and killed a popular army officer, Lieutenant Edward W. Casey, who wanted to enter the Sioux village at No Water for the purpose of talking peace. The killing appeared to be unprovoked. Plenty Horses shot Casey in the back at close quarters.

On January 11, two Sioux families, returning to Pine Ridge from hunting near Bear Butte, were ambushed by white ranchers, three brothers named Culbertson. Few Tails, the head of one of the families, was killed, and his wife was severely wounded. Somehow she made her way in the freezing cold a hundred miles to Pine Ridge. The other family—a man, his wife, and two children, one an infant—managed to reach the Rosebud Agency in two weeks. This wife, too, was wounded and weak from the loss of blood. She survived, but the infant child had died of starvation on the way.

On January 15 the Sioux leaders surrendered and established themselves at Pine Ridge Agency. The peace for which General Nelson A. Miles had worked so hard was achieved. The Indians assumed that Plenty Horses would go free, and indeed General Miles was reluctant to disturb the peace. But there were strong feelings among the soldiers. Casey had been shot in cold blood while acting in the interest of peace. On February 19, Plenty Horses was quietly arrested and removed from the reservation to Fort Meade, near Sturgis, South Dakota.

On March 27, General Miles ordered Plenty Horses released to stand trial in the federal district court at Sioux Falls. Interest ran high, and the courtroom was filled with onlookers of every description. The Plenty Horses trial was one of the most interesting and unlikely in the history of the West. Eventually the outcome turned upon the question of perception, of whether or not a state of war existed between the Sioux and the United States. If Plenty Horses and Casey were belligerents in a state of war, the defense argued, then the killing could not be considered a criminal offense, subject to trial in the civil courts.

General Miles was sensitive to this question for two reasons in particular. First, his rationale for bringing troops upon the scene—and he had amassed the largest concentration of troops in one place since the Civil War—was predicated upon the existence of a state of war. When the question was put to him directly, he replied, "It was a war. You do not suppose that I am going to reduce my campaign to a dress-parade affair?" Second, Miles had to confront the logically related corollary to the defense argument that, if no state of war existed, all the soldiers who took part in the Wounded Knee affair were guilty of murder under the law.

Miles sent a staff officer, Captain Frank D. Baldwin, to testify on behalf of Plenty Horses' defense. This testimony proved critical, and decisive. It is a notable irony that Baldwin and the slain Casey were close friends. Surely one of the principal ironies of American history is that Plenty Horses was very likely to have been the only Indian to benefit in any way from the slaughter at Wounded Knee. Plenty Horses was acquitted. So too—a final irony—were the Culbertson brothers; with Plenty Horses' acquittal, there was neither a logical basis nor a practical possibility to hold them accountable for the ambush of Few Tails and his party.

We might ponder Plenty Horses at trial, a young man sitting silent under the scrutiny of curious onlookers, braving his fate with apparent indifference. Behind the mask of a warrior was a lost and agonized soul.

As a boy Plenty Horses had been sent to Carlisle Indian School in Pennsylvania, the boarding school founded in 1879 by Richard Henry Pratt, whose obsession was to "kill the Indian and save the man." Carlisle was the model upon which an extensive system of boarding schools for Indians was based. The schools were prisons in effect, where Indian children were exposed to brutalities, sometimes subtle, sometimes not, in the interest of converting them to the white man's way of life. It was a grand experiment in ethnic cleansing and psychological warfare, and it failed. But it exacted a terrible cost upon the mental, physical, and spiritual health of Indian children.

Plenty Horses was for five years a pupil at Carlisle. Of his experience there he said:

> I found that the education I had received was of no benefit to me. There was no chance to get employment, nothing for me to do whereby I could earn my board and clothes, no opportunity to learn more and remain with the whites. It disheartened me and I went back to live as I had before going to school.

But when Plenty Horses returned to his own people, they did not fully accept him. He had lost touch with the old ways; he had lived among whites, and the association had diminished him. He rejected the white world, but he had been exposed to it, and it had left its mark upon him. And in the process he had been dislodged, uprooted from the Indian world. He could not quite get back to it. His very being had become tentative; he lived in a kind of limbo, a state of confusion, depression, and desperation.

At the trial Plenty Horses was remarkably passive. He said nothing, nor did he give any sign of his feelings. It was as if he were not there. It came later to light that he was convinced beyond any question that he would be hanged. He could not understand what was happening around him. But in a strange way he could appreciate it. Indeed he must have been fascinated. Beneath his inscrutable expression, his heart must have been racing. He was the center of a ritual, a sacrificial victim; the white man must dispose of him according to some design in the white man's universe. This was perhaps a ritual of atonement. The whites would take his life, but in the proper way, according to their notion of propriety and the appropriate. Perhaps they were involving him in their very notion of the sacred. He could only accept what was happening, and only in their terms. With silence, patience, and respect he must await the inevitable. He said later:

I am an Indian. Five years I attended Carlisle and was educated in the ways of the white man...I was lonely. I shot the lieutenant so I might make a place for myself among my people. Now I am one of them. I shall be hung and the Indians will bury me as a warrior. They will be proud of me. I am satisfied.

But Plenty Horses was not hanged, nor did he make an acceptable place for himself among his people. He was acquitted. Plenty Horses lived out his life between two worlds, without a place in either.

Perhaps the most tragic aspect of Plenty Horses' plight was his silence, the theft of his language, and the theft of meaning itself from his ordeal. At Carlisle he had been made to speak English, and his native Lakota was forbidden—thrown away, to use a term that indicates particular misfortune in the plains oral tradition. To be "thrown away" is to be negated, excluded, eliminated. After five years Plenty Horses had not only failed to master the English language, he had lost some critical possession of his native tongue as well. He was therefore crippled in his speech, wounded in his intelligence. In him was a terrible urgency to express himself—his anger and hurt, his sorrow and loneliness. But his voice was broken. In terms of his culture and all it held most sacred, Plenty Horses himself was thrown away.

In order to understand the true nature of Plenty Horses' ordeal—and a central reality in the cultural conflict that has defined the way we historically see the American West—we must first understand something about the nature of words, about the way we live our daily lives in the element of language. For in a profound sense our language determines us; it shapes our most fundamental selves; it establishes our identity and confirms our existence, our human being. Without language we are lost, "thrown away." Without names—and language is essentially a system of naming—we cannot truly claim to be.

To think is to talk to oneself. That is to say, language and thought are practically indivisible. But there is complexity in language, and there are many languages. Indeed, there are hundreds of Native American languages on the North American continent alone, many of them in the American West. As there are different languages, there are different ways of thinking. In terms of worldview, there are common denominators of experience which unify language communities to some extent. Although the Pueblo peoples of the Rio Grande Valley speak different languages, their experience of the land in which they live and have lived for thousands of years is by and large the same. And their worldview is the same. Other peoples—Europeans, for example—also have common denominators which unify them. But the difference between Native American and European worldviews is vast. And that difference is crucial to the story of the American West. We are talking about different ways of thinking, deeply different ways of looking at the world.

The oral tradition of the American Indian is a highly developed realization of language. In certain ways it is superior to the written tradition. In the oral tradition words are sacred; they are intrinsically powerful and beautiful. By means of words, by the exertion of language upon the unknown, the best of the possible—and indeed the seemingly impossible—is accomplished. Nothing exists beyond the influence of words. Words are the names of Creation. To give one's word is to give oneself, wholly—to place a name, than which nothing is more sacred, in the balance. One stands for his word; his word stands for him. The oral tradition demands the greatest clarity of speech and hearing, the whole strength of memory, and an absolute faith in the efficacy of language. Every word spoken, every word heard, is the utterance of prayer.

Thus, in the oral tradition, language bears the burden of the sacred, the burden of belief. In a written tradition, the place of language is not so certain.

Those European immigrants who ventured into the Wild West were of a written tradition, even the many who were illiterate. Their way of seeing and thinking was determined by the invention of an alphabet, the advent of the printed word, and the manufacture of books. These were great landmarks of civilization, to be sure, but they were also a radical departure from the oral tradition and an understanding of language that was inestimably older and closer to the origin of words. Although the first Europeans venturing into the continent took with them and held dear the Bible, Bunyan, and Shakespeare, their children ultimately could take words for granted, throw them away. Words, multiplied and diluted to inflation, would be preserved on shelves forever. But in this departure was also the dilution of the sacred, and the loss of a crucial connection with the real, that plane of possibility that is always larger than our comprehension. What follows such loss is overlay, imposition, the distorted view of the West of which we have been speaking.

V

My children, when at first I liked the whites,
My children, when at first I liked the whites,
I gave them fruits,
I gave them fruits.
　　　　　—ARAPAHO

Restore my voice for me.
　　　　　—NAVAJO

The landscape of the American West has to be seen to be believed. And perhaps, conversely, it has to be believed in order to be seen. Here is the confluence of image and imagination. I am a writer and a painter. I am therefore interested in what it is to see, how seeing is accomplished, how the physical eye and the mind's eye are related, how the act of seeing is or can be expressed in art and in language, and how these things are sacred in nature, as I believe them to be.

Belief is the burden of seeing. And language bears the burden of belief rightly. To see into the heart of something is to believe in it. In order to see to this extent, to see and to accomplish belief in the seeing, one must be prepared. The preparation is a spiritual exercise.

In order to be perceived in its true character, the landscape of the American West must be seen in terms of its sacred dimension. *Sacred* and *sacrifice* are related. Something is made sacred by means of sacrifice;

that which is sacred is earned. I have a friend who wears on a string around his neck a little leather pouch. In the pouch is a pebble from the creekbed at Wounded Knee. Wounded Knee is sacred ground, for it was purchased with blood. It is the site of a terrible human sacrifice. It is appropriate that my friend should keep the pebble close to the center of his being, that he should see the pebble and beyond the pebble to the battlefield and beyond the battlefield to the living earth.

The history of the West, that is, the written story that begins with the record of European intervention, is informed by tensions which arise from a failure to see the West in terms of the sacred. The oral history, the oral tradition that came before the written chronicles, is all too often left out of the equation. Yet one of the essential realities of the West is centered in this still-living past. When Europeans came into the West they encountered a people who had been there for untold millennia, for whom the landscape was a kind of cathedral of their spiritual life, the home of their deepest being. It had been earned by sacrifice forever. But the encounter was determined by a distortion of image and imagination and language, by a failure to see and believe.

George Armstrong Custer could see and articulate the beauty of the plains, but he could not see the people who inhabited them. Or he could see them only as enemies, impediments to the glory for which he hungered. He could not understand the sacred ceremony, the significance of the marriage he was offered, nor could he hear the words of warning, or comprehend their meaning.

Buffalo Bill was a plainsman, but the place he might have held on the picture plane of the West was severely compromised and ultimately lost to the theatrical pretensions of the Wild West Show. Neither did he see the Indians. What he saw at last was a self-fabricated reflection of himself and of the landscape in which he had lived a former life.

The vision of Plenty Horses was that of reunion with his traditional world. He could not realize his vision, for his old way of seeing was stolen from him in the white man's school. Ironically, just like the European emigrants, Plenty Horses attempted by his wordless act of violence to persist in his cultural being, to transform the landscape to accommodate his presence once more, to save himself. He could not do so. I believe that he wanted more than anything to pray, to make a prayer in the old way to the old deities of the world into which he was born. But I believe too that he had lost the words, that without language he could no longer bear the burden of belief.

The sun's beams are running out
The sun's beams are running out
The sun's yellow rays are running out
The sun's yellow rays are running out

We shall live again
We shall live again
    —Comanche

They will appear—may you behold them!
They will appear—may you behold them!
A horse nation will appear.
A thunder-being nation will appear.
They will appear, behold!
They will appear, behold!
      —Kiowa

part two

ESSAYS IN PLACE

Introduction

The events of one's life take place, take place. *How often have I used that expression, and how often have I stopped to think what it means? Events do indeed take place; they have meaning in relation to the things around them.*

—THE NAMES

Where words and place come together, there is the sacred. The question "Where are you going?" is so commonplace in so many languages that it has the status of a universal greeting; it is formulaic. There is an American folksong that begins,

> *Well, where do you come from,*
> *And where do you go?*
> *Well, where do you come from,*
> *My cotton-eye Joe?*

The questions are so familiar that they are taken for granted. But their implications, their consequent meanings, are profound. In the deepest matter of these words are the riddles of origin and destiny, and by extension the stuff of story and ritual. *I belong in the place of my departure,* says Odysseus, *and I belong in the place that is my destination.* Only in this spectrum is the quest truly possible. The sense of place and the sense of belonging are bonded fast by the imagination. And words, in all their formal and informal manifestations, are the best espression of the imagination.

Linguists have long suggested that we are determined by our native language, that language defines and confines us. It may be so. The definition and confinement do not concern me beyond a certain point, for I believe that language in general is practically without limits. We are not in danger of exceeding the boundaries of language, nor are we prisoners of language in any dire way. I am much more concerned with *my* place within the context of *my* language. This, I think, must be a principle of storytelling. And the storyteller's place within the context of his language must include both a geographical and mythic frame of reference. Within that frame of reference is the freedom of infinite possibility. The place of infinite possibility is where the storyteller belongs.

Sacred Places

There is a place, a round, trampled patch of the red earth, near Carnegie, Oklahoma, where the Kiowa Gourd Dances were held in the early years of the century. When my father was six or eight years old, my grandfather, who was a member of the *Tian-paye*, or Gourd Dance Society, took him there. In one of the intervals of the dance there was a "giveaway," an ancient Plains tradition of giving gifts as a public expression of honor and esteem. My grandfather's name was called, and he let go of my father's hand and strode out upon the dance ground. Then a boy about my father's age led a black hunting horse, prancing and blowing, into the circle and placed the reins in my grandfather's hands, still warm with my father's touch. The great muscles of the horse rippled in light, and bright ribbons were fixed in its mane and tail. My father watched in wonder and delight, his heart bursting with excitement and pride. And when he told me of that moment, as he did a number of times because I craved to hear it, I could see it as vividly as if I had been there. The brilliant image of that moment remained in my father's mind all his life, as it remains in mine. It is a thing that related him and relates me to the sacred earth.

> *This afternoon is older*
> *than the giving of gifts*
> *and the rhythmic scraping of the red earth.*
> *My father's father's name is called,*
> *and the gift horse stutters out, whole,*
> *and the whole horizon is in its eyes.*
> *In the giveaway is beaded*

the blood memories of fathers and sons.
Oh, there is nothing like this afternoon
in all the miles and years around,
and I am not here,
but, grandfather, father, I am here.

To encounter the sacred is to be alive at the deepest center of human existence. Sacred places are the truest definitions of the earth; they stand for the earth immediately and forever; they are its flags and shields. If you would know the earth for what it really is, learn it through its sacred places. At Devil's Tower or Canyon de Chelly or the Cahokia Mounds you touch the pulse of the living planet; you feel its breath upon you. You become one with a spirit that pervades geologic time, that indeed confounds time and space. When I stand on the edge of Monument Valley and behold the great red and blue and purple monoliths floating in the distance, I have the certain sense that I see beyond time. There the earth lies in eternity.

Sacred ground is in some way earned. It is consecrated, made holy with offerings—song and ceremony, joy and sorrow, the dedication of the mind and heart, offerings of life and death. The words "sacred" and "sacrifice" are related.

Acts of sacrifice make sacred the earth. Language and the sacred are indivisible. The earth and all its appearances and expressions exist in names and stories and prayers and spells. North American place names are a sacred music: Medicine Wheel, Bear Butte, Bobaquiveri, Chaco, Sleeping Ute, Lukachukai, Wounded Knee.

Mircea Eliade has said that the sacred, in all times, is "the revelation of the real, an encounter with that which saves us by giving meaning to our existence." Yes, I want to say, here is a brilliant equation of the sacred with reality, salvation, and meaning. But there is more, for the sacred finally transcends definition. The mind does not comprehend it; it is at last to be recognized and acknowledged in the heart and soul. Those who seek to study or understand the sacred in academic terms are misled. The sacred is not a discipline. It is a dimension beyond the ordinary and beyond the mechanics of analysis. For those who come to the sacred, to sacred ground, it is a kind of mystical experience, a deep and singular encounter.

Sacred ground is ground that is invested with belief. Belief, at its root, exists independent of meaning. That is, its expression and object may escape what we can perceive as definable meaning. The intrinsic power of sacred ground is often ineffable and abstract. I behold a particular sacred place, the great gallery of rock paintings at Barrier Canyon, Utah, for example. There on the massive wall are large, sharply defined works of art, anthropomorphic figures in procession. They image ceremony in its ultimate expression: humans, or humanlike gods, engaged in the drama of *being*. They perform the verb "to be." They reflect the human condition; they signify humanity in all places at all times. They proceed from the depths of origin, from a genesis nearly beyond the reach of imagination.

The figures in the eternal procession at Barrier Canyon are related to us in story. We do not know the story, but we see its enactment on the face of the earth, that it reaches from the beginning of time to the present to a destiny beyond time. We do not know what the story means, but more importantly we know *that* it means, and that we are deeply involved in its meaning. The sacred is profoundly mysterious, and our belief in it is no less profound.

In Native American oral tradition the reverence which humans have for the earth is a story told many times in many places in many languages. Speaking of aged men and women on the northern plains, Luther Standing Bear said:

> It was good for the skin to touch the earth, and the old people liked to remove their moccasins and walk with bare feet on the sacred earth. The birds that flew in the air came to rest upon the earth and it was the final abiding place of all things that lived and grew. The soil was soothing, strengthening, cleansing and healing.

A prayer from the Night Chant of the Navajo begins with homage to *Tsegi!*, "place among the rocks," place of origin. It would be impossible

to imagine an invocation of greater moment or power, or a word or
concept more elemental.

> *House made of dawn,*
> *House made of evening light,*
> *House made of dark cloud,*
> *House made of male rain,*
> *House made of dark mist,*
> *House made of female rain,*
> *House made of pollen,*
> *House made of grasshoppers,*
> *Dark Cloud is at the door.*
> *The trail out of it is dark cloud.*
> *The zigzag lightning stands high upon it.*

But where there is the sacred there is sacrilege, the theft of the sacred.
To steal the sacred is to rob us of our very selves, our reason for being,
our being itself. And sacrilege is a sin of which we are capable. Look
around you.

When I was a small boy there was a box of bones in the barn of my
Kiowa homestead on Rainy Mountain Creek, where I loved to go and
visit my grandmother. They were the bones of a horse, a legendary
hunter, a horse of exceptional speed and endurance. The horse belonged
to my grandfather, who owned many horses, and who died before I was
born. The bones were for me a tangible link to my heritage. They were
sacred. Their very existence made of the barn a singular place, a shrine.
Then one day I went there, and the box of bones was gone. Alarmed,
I went to my grandmother, who whispered to me that the bones had
been stolen. Even as a child I knew an unnamable sadness, a sense of
loss that would from that moment adhere to my heart.

The sacred places of North America are threatened, even as the sacred
earth is threatened. In my generation we have taken steps—small, tentative steps—to preserve forests and rivers and animals. We must also,
and above all, take steps to preserve the spiritual centers of our earth,

those places that are invested with the dreams of our ancestors and the well-being of our children.

It is good for us, too, to touch the earth. We, and our children, need the chance to walk the sacred earth, this final abiding place of all that lives. We must preserve our sacred places in order to know our place in time, our reach to eternity.

Revisiting Sacred Ground

There is great good in returning to a landscape that has had extraordinary meaning in one's life. It happens that we return to such places in our minds irresistibly. There are certain villages and towns, mountains and plains that, having seen them, walked in them, lived in them, even for a day, we keep forever in the mind's eye. They become indispensable to our well-being; they define us, and we say, I am who I am because I have been there, or there. There is good, too, in actual, physical return.

Some years ago I made a pilgrimage into the heart of North America. I began the journey proper in western Montana. From there I traveled across the high plains of Wyoming into the Black Hills, then southward to the southern plains, to a cemetery at Rainy Mountain, in Oklahoma. It was a journey made by my Kiowa ancestors long before. In the course of their migration they became a people of the Great Plains, and theirs was the last culture to evolve in North America. They had been for untold generations a mountain tribe of hunters. Their ancient nomadism, which had determined their way of life even before they set foot on this continent, perhaps thirty thousand years ago, was raised to its highest level of expression when they entered upon the Great Plains and acquired horses. Their migration brought them to a golden age. At the beginning of their journey they were a people of hard circumstances, often hungry and cold, fighting always for sheer survival. At its end, and for a hundred years, they were the lords of the land, a daring race of centaurs and buffalo hunters whose love of freedom and space was profound.

Recently I returned to the old migration route of the Kiowas. I had in me a need to behold again some of the principal landmarks of that long, prehistoric quest, to descend again from the mountain to the plain.

With my close friend Chuck I drove north to the Montana–Wyoming border. I wanted to intersect the Kiowa migration route at the Bighorn Medicine Wheel, high in the Bighorn Mountains. We gradually ascended to eight thousand feet on a well-maintained but winding highway. Then we climbed sharply, bearing upon timberline. It was early October, and although the plain below had been comfortable, even warm at midday, the mountain air was cold, and much of the ground was covered with snow. We turned off the pavement, on a dirt road that led three miles to the Medicine Wheel. The road was forbidding; it was narrow and winding, and the grades were steep and slippery; here and there the shoulders fell away into deep ravines. But at the same time something wonderful happened: we crossed the line between civilization and wilderness. Suddenly the earth persisted in its original being. Directly in front of us a huge white-tailed buck crossed our path, ambling without haste into a thicket of pines. As we drove over his tracks we saw four does above on the opposite bank, looking down at us, their great black eyes bright and benign, curious. There seemed no wariness, nothing of fear or alienation. Their presence was a good omen, we thought; somehow in their attitude they bade us welcome to their sphere of wildness.

There was a fork in the road, and we took the wrong branch. At a steep, hairpin curve we got out of the car and climbed to the top of a peak. An icy wind whipped at us; we were among the bald summits of the Bighorns. Great flumes of sunlit snow erupted on the ridges and dissolved in spangles on the sky. Across a deep saddle we caught sight of the Medicine Wheel. It was perhaps two miles away.

When we returned to the car we saw another vehicle approaching. It was a very old Volkswagen bus, in much need of repair, cosmetic repair at least. Out stepped a thin, bearded young man in thick glasses. He wore a wool cap, a down parka, jeans, and well-worn hiking boots. "I am looking for Medicine Wheel," he said, having nodded to us. He spoke softly, with a pronounced accent. His name was Jurg, and he was from Switzerland; he had been traveling for some months in Canada and the United States. Chuck and I shook his hand and told him to follow us, and we drove down into the saddle. From there we climbed on foot to the Medicine Wheel.

The Medicine Wheel is a ring of stones, some fifty feet in diameter. Stone spokes radiate from the center to the circumference. Cairns are placed at certain points on the circumference, one in the center, and one just outside the ring to the southwest. We do not know as a matter of fact who made the wheel or to what purpose. It has been proposed that it is an astronomical observatory, a solar calendar, and the ground design of a Kiowa Sun Dance lodge. What we know without doubt is that it is a sacred expression, an equation of man's relation to the cosmos.

There was a great calm upon that place. The hard, snow-bearing wind that had burned our eyes and skin only minutes before had died away altogether. The sun was warm and bright, and there was a profound silence. On the wire fence which had been erected to enclose and protect the wheel were fixed offerings, small prayer bundles. Chuck and Jurg and I walked about slowly, standing for long moments here and there, looking into the wheel or out across the great distances. We did not say much; there was little to be said. But we were deeply moved by the spirit of that place. The silence was such that it must be observed. To the north we could see down to timberline, to the snowfields and draws that marked the black planes of forest among the peaks of the Bighorns. To the south and west the mountains fell abruptly to the plains. We could see thousands of feet down and a hundred miles across the dim expanse.

When we were about to leave, I took from my pocket an eagle-bone whistle that my father had given me, and I blew it in the four directions. The sound was very high and shrill, and it did not break the essential silence. As we were walking down we saw far below, crossing our path, a coyote sauntering across the snow into a wall of trees. It was just there, a wild being to catch sight of, and then it was gone. The wilderness, which had admitted us with benediction, with benediction let us go.

When we came within a stone's throw of the highway, Chuck and I said goodbye to Jurg, but not before he had got out his camp stove and boiled water for tea. There in the dusk we enjoyed a small ceremonial feast of tea and crackers. The three of us had become friends. Only later did I begin to understand the extraordinary character of that friendship. It was the friendship of those who come together in recognition of the sacred. If we never meet again, I thought, we shall not forget this day.

On the plains the fences and roads and windmills and houses seemed almost negligible, all but overwhelmed by the earth and sky. It is a landscape of great clarity; its vastness is that of the ocean. It is the near revelation of infinity. Antelope were everywhere in the grassy folds, grazing side by side with horses and cattle. Hawks sailed above, and crows scattered before us. The place names were American—Tensleep, Buffalo, Dull Knife, Crazy Woman, Spotted Horse.

The Black Hills are an isolated and ancient group of mountains in South Dakota and Wyoming. They lie very close to both the geographic center of the United States, if you include Alaska and Hawaii, and the geographic center of the North American continent. They form an island, an elliptical area of nearly six thousand square miles, in the vast sea of grasses that is the northern Great Plains. The Black Hills are a calendar of geologic time that is truly remarkable. Their foundation rocks are much older than the sedimentary layers of which the Americas are primarily formed. An analysis of this foundation, made in 1964, indicates an age of between two and three billion years.

A documented record of exploration in this region is found in the Lewis and Clark journals, 1804–1806. The first white party known definitely to have entered the Black Hills proper was led by Jedidiah Smith in 1823. The diary of this expedition, kept by one James Clyman, is notable. Clyman reports a confrontation between Jedidiah Smith and a grizzly bear, in which Smith lost one of his ears. There is also reported the discovery of a petrified ("putrified," as Clyman has it) forest in which petrified birds sing petrified songs.

The Lakotas, or Teton Sioux, called these mountains *Paha Sapa*, "hills that are black." Other tribes, beside the Kiowas and the Sioux, thought of the Black Hills as sacred ground, a place that is crucial in their past. The Arapahos lived here. So did the Cheyennes. Bear Butte, near Sturgis, South Dakota, on the northeast edge of the Black Hills, is the Cheyennes' sacred mountain. It remains, like the Medicine Wheel, a place of the greatest spiritual intensity. So great was thought to be the power inherent in the Black Hills that the Indians did not camp there. It was a place of rendezvous, a hunting ground, but above all an inviolate, sacred ground. It was a place of thunder and lightning, a dwelling place of the gods.

On the edge of the Black Hills nearest the Bighorn Mountains is Devil's Tower, the first of our national monuments. The Lakotas called it *Mateo Tepee,* "Grizzly Bear Lodge." The Kiowas called it *Tsoai,* "Rock Tree." Devil's Tower is a great monolith that rises high above the timber of the Black Hills. In conformation it closely resembles the stump of a tree. It is a cluster of rock columns of phonolite porphyry 1,000 feet across at the base and 275 feet across at the top. It rises 865 feet above the high ground upon which it stands and 1,280 feet above the Belle Fourche River, which runs in the valley below.

It has to be seen to be believed. "There are things in nature that engender an awful quiet in the heart of man; Devil's Tower is one of them." I wrote these words almost twenty years ago. They remain true to my experience. Each time I behold this *Tsoai* anew I am more than ever in awe of it.

Two hundred years ago, more or less, the Kiowas came upon this place. They were moved to tell a story about it:

> Eight children were there at play, seven sisters and their brother. Suddenly the boy was struck dumb; he trembled and began to run upon his hands and feet. His fingers became claws, and his body was covered with fur. Directly there was a bear where the boy had been. The sisters were terrified; they ran, and the bear after them. They came to the stump of a great tree, and the tree spoke to them. It bade them climb upon it, and as they did so it began to rise into the air. The bear came to kill them, but they were just beyond its reach. It reared against the tree and scored the bark all around with its claws. The seven sisters were borne into the sky, and they became the stars of the Big Dipper.

This story, which I have known from the time I could first understand language, exemplifies the sacred for me. The storyteller, that anonymous, man who told the story for the first time, succeeded in raising the human condition to the level of universal significance. Not only did he account for the existence of the rock tree, but in the process he related his people to the stars.

When Chuck and I had journeyed over this ground together, when we were about to go our separate ways, I reminded him of our friend Jurg, knowing well enough that I needn't have; Jurg was on our minds. I can't account for it. He had touched us deeply with his trust, not unlike that of the wild animals we had seen, and with his generosity of spirit, his concern to see beneath the surface of things, his attitude of free, clear, direct, disinterested kindness.

"Did he tell us what he does?" I asked. "Does he have a profession?"
"I don't think he said," Chuck replied. "I think he's a pilgrim."
"Yes."
"Yes."

Navajo Place-Names

Where language touches the earth, there is the holy, there is the sacred. In our deepest intelligence we know this: that names and being are indivisible. That which has no name cannot truly be said to exist, to be. That which bears a name bears being as well. *I have a name; therefore I am.* And, of course, there is a wonderful particularity in names. If we are speaking of place, which is (or ought to be) a fundamental concept in our lives, the particularity is critical. We know who we are (and where we are) only with reference to the things about us, the points of reference in both our immediate and infinite worlds, the places and points among which we are born, grow old, and die. There is in this simple cartology the idea of odyssey. And in odyssey there is story. Nothing appeals more to our human being.

"Where is Haske?"

"Haske has gone to Gallup."

"Ah, *Na'nizhoozhi*, the place of the bridge."

"*A'oo*, the bridge over the Rio Puerco. It has long been a meeting place for the *Dine*."

"When I was a child at *Ch'inili* I thought of *Na'nizhoozhi* as one of the great cities of the world."

"And so it is. There is no world without the lights of *Na'nizhoozhi*. Haske has gone there to meet a man from *Naakai To*, a man who owns fine horses, they say."

"There is a story in that, *daats'i*."

"We are talking about horses. We are telling a story."

The Navajos say of their language, *Dine bizaad,* "it is endless." I realized the truth of this saying when I studied the language with Alan Wilson in the early seventies. Although I am not Navajo, I had lived at Shiprock, Tuba City, and Chinle as a child. I had heard the sounds of the Navajo language, its rhythms and inflections, its cadences and pitches, at a fortunate time, when my ear was more alive to the spoken word than it had ever been or would ever be again. When I met Alan and came into the immediate presence of the Navajo language again, I found that *Dine bizaad* was alive in my memory and in my hearing.

What a joy it was to enter again into that particular dimension of sound and meaning! But I knew next to nothing about the logical structure of the language. The great grammar of Navajo was completely new to me, and yet I had the advantage of knowing something about its oral underpinnings. With Alan's help, I began to perceive the patterns and geometries of Navajo. I began to see that Navajo was indeed endless. *Dine bizaad.*

One day a remarkable thing happened. I was driving from Gallup north toward Kayenta. Soon there appeared on the side of the road a young Navajo hitchhiker, certainly not unusual there and then. I pulled over, and he climbed into the car. He nodded his thanks in a very jovial manner. He was clearly grateful to be given the lift, and he seemed to be at home in the world. I started talking to him in my meager, broken Navajo. He was amused, I'm sure, but he was gracious. He did not want to embarrass me; even so, he could not help drawing me quickly below my depth. But I had a basic question: *Ei hash hoolye?* "What is the name of that place," or "How is that place called?" I must have asked this question a hundred times, and a hundred times he had the name of the place I pointed out.

"*Ei hash hoolye?*"

"*Tse Awa'e.*"

"What is that place?"

"Rock babies."

"*Ei hash hoolye?*"

"*To Dineeshzhee.*"

"What is that place?"

"Water fanning out, water spreading in rivulets."

I was amazed. It became slowly clear to me that this man was indeed *at home*. He was eminently familiar with the places that defined him. Not only did he know them, as we know the images of cityscape, horizon, and, if we are truly blessed, the stars in the night sky, but he knew their *names!*

One day Alan, and I drove into Monument Valley, *Tse Bii' Ndzisgaii*, and camped for the night in a box canyon, under an overhanging red cliff that rode in the sky at every hour of the day and night. It seemed always to be in motion, and it was something for the imagination, something for the hungry spirit. Beyond the mouth of our canyon there were the Three Sisters, those slender monuments, statuary of an ancient deity, that seem to defy erosion and gravity. Above us were the brightest stars I have ever seen. We built a fire and cooked an incomparable meal. The good-smelling smoke of our fire rose slowly upon the incline of the great wall leaning over us, great, mythic shadows rising there as if in the telling of a primal story. We slept deeply, deeply in that place.

The next morning we awoke and breakfasted in the wonder of the world. Then we climbed to the end of the canyon, to a window-shaped opening high above the canyon floor. And through the window we saw the vast valley below, reaching out across the long, sacred expanse of the continent. In the distance under us there were two men on horseback, Navajo men going in slow motion toward story, toward a memory that would keep to my mind forever. They were singing a riding song, and the song rose up to us with the clarity of a bell. Somewhere in the back of my mind I knew then and there that the essential things of the world and the universe are in place, *in place*. They are fixed forever in their names.

Sacred Images

The art of prehistoric times, especially rock paintings and engravings, is of special interest to me, for I believe that it is an essential element in the determination and appreciation of our human experience. As a painter, I am concerned to understand the relationship between the artist and his subject, for that relationship is ancient and sacred. To understand that relationship, even imperfectly, gives us a way to find our place in the world, to reckon the course of our journey from birth to death and from Genesis to the edge of time and beyond. As a writer, I am fascinated by language, and I am aware that drawing and painting—the act of setting an image upon a plane—is primarily an expression, an assertion of language.

The great student of mythology, Joseph Campbell, wrote that "it is only from the insights of its own creative seers and artists that any people has ever derived its appropriate, life-supporting, and maturing myths and rites." In prehistoric art, we confront the symbols of our being. We venture upon the unknown. We touch the sacred, and we do so with dread, holy dread. Perhaps that is our most human and creative emotion.

I was recently in Spain. My official purpose was to read a paper on Jorge Luis Borges to a society of writers in Granada. But my passion was to visit the Altamira caves. I wanted to see those magnificent animals grazing on the ceiling. I wanted to see them as the nine-year-old Maria Sanz de Sautuola had seen them in 1879.

This is the story: Marcelino Sanz de Sautuola was a young gentleman of Santander, a man of science, especially interested in prehistory. A sharecropper on his summer estate of Puente de San Miguel told Don

Marcelino that he had discovered a cave nearby. Don Marcelino visited the cave in 1875, saw a few unremarkable paintings, and was not excited by them. This was another cave in a landscape riddled with caves.

Four years later Don Marcelino returned for the second time to Altamira, this time accompanied by his daughter, Maria. By the light of a carbide lamp, they entered the room which is now known as the Hall of the Bisons, and it was Maria who first noticed the low ceiling, stained with ocher, which covered the whole vault. There were the strange animals, grazing in eternity. They emerged from a blackness unimaginable, seemingly alive, moving in the flickering light. Maria was the first person to see them in seventeen thousand years.

And so, I came to Altamira. I passed through a small green door on a hillside in Cantabria. It was a passage from time into timelessness. There are the paintings of animals—bison, boar, horse, deer, goat. You look at them, and you know that they were placed there by an artist or artists who loved them, in whom they inspired wonder and awe and reverence. As much as did the buffalo and the horse to the Plains Indian of the nineteenth century, they extended his human being to the center of wilderness, of mystery, of deepest life itself. Like the paintings of the greatest artists of every age, they are so fundamental as to be profound.

In 1995 the French government announced the discovery of a Paleolithic cave, near Avignon, by a local official, Jean-Marie Chauvet. The 30,000-year-old paintings therein are magnificent. Again, there are animals, but unlike the pastoral creatures at Altamira, these are fierce, dangerous, frightening. Here are woolly rhinoceroses, cave bears, and lions. One can speculate about the Altamira artist: he knew these animals, and he loved them; they were his sacred access to the world around him. Of the Chauvet artist, one can speculate: he knew these animals, and he feared them. No less did he love and respect them. They were deities, or they were the emissaries of deities. They were sacred.

And on the North American continent, in the Southwest, we have the rock art at Barrier Canyon, at Books Cliffs, in the Malpais, and throughout the American Southwest, where the proliferation of anthropomorphic forms speaks directly to the shamanistic and ceremonial dimensions of prehistoric art. Here are stories told. And they are stories in which we are unmistakably involved. They are not wholly intelligible (neither are the chants of the Mountain Spirits in the contemporary *yei bichai* of the Navajo), but they are deeply moving, and they emerge from the farthest reaches of our racial memory. The mysterious figures of the Great Gallery at Barrier Canyon are surely also sacred, seen by the artist with awe and holy dread. The paintings and engravings of the Southwest are at once the beginning of art in America and the beginning of American literature.

Teilhard de Chardin wrote of Altamira: "What we really discover is our own childhood, we discover ourselves [because we observe] the same essential aspirations in the depths of our souls."

I think, how fitting that a child should be the first in recorded history to see these paintings. In a real sense, these polychrome images are child's play. For these ancient images are intimately related to language, and language is child's play. None of us can master language so well as a child.

The late Lewis Thomas, speculating on the acquisition of language, wrote:

> I suggest that it began in the children, and it probably began when the earliest settlements, or the earliest nomadic tribes, reached a sufficient density of population so that there were plenty of very young children in close contact with each other, a critical mass of children, playing together all day long.
>
> When it first happened, it must have come as an overwhelming surprise to the adults. I can imagine the scene.... The children have been noisier than ever in recent weeks, especially the three- and four-year-olds. Now they begin to make a clamor never heard before, a tumult of sounds, words tumbling over words, the newest, wildest of all the human sounds ever made, rising in volume and intensity, exultant, and all of it totally incomprehensible to the adults.... In that moment, human culture was away and running.

And it must have been so with those who struggled with an alphabet, the bonding of voice and image, the translation of sound into symbol, the word made visible: imaging, imagining, incising, writing.

The dictionary definition of the word "write" that I first discovered in my undergraduate days, "to draw or form by or as by scoring or incising a surface," admits of all rock art. It enables us to see the images at Altamira, Lascaux, Chauvet, Barrier Canyon as language, as story, as a critical moment in the evolution of literature. The sense of that moment is profound. When I passed through the green door into the caves of Altamira, it was a passage from time into timelessness. I beheld myself across a chasm of time, beyond time. I was looking not only into the childhood of my finite life—recovering the wonder and delight I had known as a child—but into the dawn of my human being. I felt that I was glimpsing the infinite. I was looking into eternity.

Writing as we know it, we believe, is about six thousand years old. But suppose we argue that writing is twenty thousand, even thirty thousand years old, and we offer as evidence the drawings in the Altamira and Chauvet caves. There is no alphabet, no script, as such, no recognizable ciphers, no narrative element that we can perceive. But there are clear images on a surface, placed there by a human hand. You may say that this is a crude form of writing indeed, but so are some of the finest paintings by Picasso crude in the best sense. Picasso once remarked that he had spent a lifetime learning to paint like a child.

What we have in all writing and in all prehistoric rock art, so called, is a common denominator that is truly definitive: the element of story. Man is a storyteller. If there is no story on the ceiling at Altamira, in the paintings of Picasso, in the poems of Emily Dickinson, or in the novels of Dostoyevsky, then these things—these superb expressions of the human spirit—have no reason for being. The artists of Altamira, of Lascaux and Chauvet, of Barrier Canyon, were telling stories.

What *are* the stories of Altamira, of Lascaux, of Chauvet, of Barrier Canyon? We do not know. There are many more questions than there are answers. But let me suggest that this is as it should be. The questions are deeply creative, and they inspire the imagination. That is important, that is one of the essential aspirations of which Teilhard de Chardin spoke. In this great field of mystery, let us hold on to the wonder that excites the imagination. Let us not insist upon answers that will diminish our curiosity, that will kill our instinct for questions.

From whatever point of view, we perceive in this ancient art the first realization of art itself, and in our blood we remember our earliest experience of form, symmetry, color, depth, perspective—of beauty—and we are given again the whole and immediate gift of wonder and astonishment and delight. In these sacred images we come hard upon the confluences of instinct and thought, stasis and creativity, savagery and sensitivity, blindness and vision, the merest survival and the greatest triumph. To behold them is to see into the spiritual caverns of our evolution, which is to see into eternity. We can ask no more, and we must not ask less, of art.

Zagorsk: To the Spiritual Center of Russia

Twenty years ago I boarded on Aeroflot plane in Paris, bound for Moscow. It was my first visit to Russia, which I knew barely and irresistibly in the pages of its literature—Turgenev and Tolstoy, Dostoyevsky and Pushkin, especially Chekhov. I was full of expectation, but the expectation of what, exactly, I could not say. The sleek Ilushin airplane bore no relation at all to those troikas I had seen in my dreams, stitching precisely with the tremble of bells the moonlit snowfields below, headed for a grand evening at a grand estate. There would be lean, heavy-browed men in brilliant uniforms, beautiful women in diaphanous gowns, music, blinis and caviar, champagne and vodka without end.

The plane ascended steeply (like the escalators in the Moscow subway, I was soon to learn), with mighty force, to cruising altitude, then leveled off. Suddenly the internal atmosphere changed remarkably. A strange euphoria pervaded the cabin. There was a party. Food was broken out, food of the most delicious and rarest kind—cheeses, cold cuts, fishes in preserve, delicious breads. Bottles of vodka were opened and passed both ways across the aisle. It was a memorable flight. It was not quite the grand party of which I had dreamed, but it would do. I passed in giddiness through the Iron Curtain.

Earlier that day I had breakfasted with a friend on the Boulevard St. Germain. He had lived all his life in Paris, and he was a nearly perfect guide and source of information on the history and character of his homeland. We had been to Chartres together, and we reflected on the great cathedral there.

"It seems at least unlikely, doesn't it, that man could construct such a thing?" I said. In my mind I was standing again in the great nave, under arches that seemed to float in their own dimension of space, gazing at the brilliant stained glass windows. "How, Pierre, is it possible? Tell me."

"Well, my friend," Pierre said solemnly, after a long moment, "you know, those people, then and there, they were full of God."

The notion of a people full of God intrigued me, and it rang true to my experience. I grew up in the American Southwest, which is essentially a spiritual landscape. There is a kind of link between Chartres and the old ruin of Giusewa, say, or some of the old *moradas* of the Penitentes in northern New Mexico. One bears a spiritual baggage on his way; I was, without knowing it, preparing myself for what I would encounter in Russia.

From the first moment I set foot on Russian soil I could feel the strength of that country. I could see in that cold, hard land—in the faces of the people there—an endurance, a holding fast against great odds, that reminded me of the strength that has informed other peoples, my own Native American people included. I would come to see that this endurance, this holding fast, is a definition of the Russian people. There is in Russia a spiritual integrity that underlies all other expressions of life. What an irony that this essential quality has survived especially in the institution of religion, an institution which was suppressed by the Communist state for most of this century.

One winter evening, soon after my first arrival in Moscow, I was strolling in the Lenin Hills, now known as the Sparrow Hills, near the university. It was one of those Russian nights when the light seems to hang indefinitely in the northern sky. Suddenly the woods seemed filled with people, silhouettes moving with purpose toward the river. Curious, I fell in with them. We came to a small church, the Church of the Trinity. I went in and found myself in a setting I could not have imagined. Candles blazed everywhere, touching a golden brilliance to the icons on all the walls. Singing welled from behind the altar, not singing in any ordinary sense, but a deep, soulful celebration of song, a holy music, a reaching across worlds on the level of the human voice. People were praying aloud and crossing themselves with great animation and conviction. The priest seemed to hold a great wave of devotion in his hands, under his control. He was the conductor of a wonderful and unique and holy celebration. It remains in my mind's eye, after twenty years, as an image of absolute wonder and concentrated devotion. Here, I thought, as I beheld the faces of the celebrants, mostly old and worn with uneasy life, are a people full of God.

This year, after twenty years, I returned to Russia, and to Zagorsk, the heart of Russian Orthodoxy and, perhaps, the heart of the Russia I had found twenty years earlier, a people full of God. In the geography of religion, Zagorsk is unique. It is among the great architectural splendors of the world. Moreover, it is a sacred place, a place of profound holiness and spirituality. I am glad to be here again, after twenty years. Such places fill me with wonder and admiration; inspiration is perhaps the better word.

Zagorsk is a Soviet appellation in honor of Vladimir Zagorsky, a Party secretary blown up by a bomb in 1919. The town in which the famous monastery is situated was also known as Zagorsk, but now it is more appropriately named Serrievsky Posad. Saint Sergius of Radonezh founded the famous Trinity Monastery there about 1340. He united the country against Mongol Tatar rule and supported Dmitry Donskoy's defeat of the Tatars. Later, while Moscow was occupied by the Poles, the monastery withstood a sixteen-month siege, and it supported the uprising that drove the Poles out. As one of the forts indispensable to the security of Moscow it was designated a *lavra*, "exalted monastery," and grew enormously wealthy through the generosity of the tsars. Closed by the Bolsheviks, it was reopened after World War II as the Zagorsk Historical and Art Museum.

Now once again restored to its name, the Trinity Monastery of St. Sergius of Radonezh is undoubtedly Russia's foremost center of spiritual and national pilgrimage. And Saint Sergius, who is the patron saint of all Russia, is enshrined there. Now in my mind's eye the monastery with its great walls and towers and gleaming domes, its well-kept grounds and its priceless treasures of religious art, is not only impressive to me, a visitor from the other side of the earth, but deeply inspiring. And this inspiration is concentrated in its breathtaking architecture, but even more in the faces of the pilgrims, many of them aged and infirm, scarred and crippled by lifetimes of oppression and suffering. Their devotion is unmistakable.

On the way from Moscow to Servievsky Posad, I was full of anticipation. My earlier visit came to mind in such detail as I did not know was in my memory. As on my previous visit, it was winter when I came to Zagorsk, the Russian winter; the air was very sharp, and the sky was all day the color of pewter. On either side of the road were vast snowfields broken by long stands of black timber, and here and there villages with little houses and smoking chimneys, always more colorful than you expect, stood out of the gray expanse. The color blue is everywhere in rural Russia—especially the window frames, which are often of a blue that draws the eye irresistibly and immediately to them. It was all there again.

My old friend Alexander Vaschenko, a scholar and translator, accompanied me as my host and interpreter. We had hired a state car. It was small and uncomfortable, and it was very sluggish. Our driver was an amiable careful man in his fifties, who spoke only when spoken to, but he was more than ready to converse as we wished. When we arrived at the monastery, Alexander told me to wait while he went into the rectory to announce our arrival. He had phoned earlier to arrange for someone to be on hand to show us around and answer our questions. The driver and I, having no language in common, sat in a kind of embarrassed silence. But after a few moments he turned to me with enthusiasm. Then from the glove compartment he produced a small chess set, of the pegs-in-holes kind, and signed me an invitation to play. I accepted. By the time Alexander returned I had lost several pieces, and my queen was in grave danger. I was grateful for the early end to the game.

Alexander and I were welcomed by Father Iov, director of the Department of Pilgrimage. He ushered us into a kind of conference room, and we talked about the history and organization of the monastery. He explained that there are 160 monks, more or less, in residence at any given time. A large number of these, remarkably, are novices. Father Iov talked about Saint Sergius of Radonezh, who was born on May 3, 1314, and founded the monastery 650 years ago. He told us that the body of Saint Sergius, which suffered no decay after death, is preserved in the

Troitsky Sobor, the Trinity Cathedral, which is the soul of the monastery, and indeed the soul of Russia. Pilgrims come from all corners
of the country and abroad to worship and kiss the sacred relics.

We had lunch. Father Iov and Alexander and I were served a wonderful borscht with dense, moist bread, thick fruitcakes, and a delicious
black tea sweetened with jam. It was no doubt the kind of fare that had
been served in the monastery for centuries.

Father Iov assigned a novice, Sergei, who had lived in San Francisco
and who spoke English fluently, to give us a tour of the monastery. I
could not have wished for a better guide. Sergei reminded me of a man
I had heard in the Cathedral of Chartres leading a small group of English
speakers through that magnificent edifice. Overhearing him, I had tagged
along. Very soon it became clear that the cathedral was his great passion,
that he had invested much of his life in researching it, and that he knew
more about it than most people can hope to learn in a lifetime. Sergei
was of that same dedication, and in spite of his youth, his knowledge
was profound.

With patience and great good will, Sergei led us first to the Trinity
Cathedral, which is not only the heart of Russian Orthodoxy, but also
the repository of great Russian art. Many of its icons were painted by
Andrey Rublyov and his students, and its iconostasis is perhaps the most
beautiful and important in the world. At its center was Rublyov's famous
painting of the Trinity, which is now in the Tretyakov Gallery in Moscow. It has been replaced in the iconostasis by a copy, but even the
copy, in lamplight, in the dark, glittering interior of the cathedral, trans-
fixes the viewer. The three seated figures are perfectly balanced in relation
to the golden bowl at their hands. Their gowns are translucent. The
hands and feet are between realism and representation; their heads are
bent in an attitude of piety and contemplation. They sit stiffly in chairs
that are nearly rounded in shape, with wings and feet. We are looking
at something that proceeds not from the mind only, but from the heart
and soul. Rublyov's *Trinity* has been for five centuries one of the great
treasures of the world. In the Tretyakov Gallery it is a masterpiece. In
the Trinity Cathedral, in the presence of most holy relics, it must have
been, even as its copy is, part and parcel of the divine.

I paused for a long time before the iconostasis, touched with my hands and lips the casket which contains the relics of Saint Sergius, listened to the voices of the pilgrims, inhaled the pungent odors of incense, garlic, oil smoke, and Russian soap, and gazed upon the glistening surfaces of holy art. The casket and iconostasis were lighted by oil lamps only. There was singing and chanting, and the constant rumble—swelling, falling, piercing—of prayer, floating in the brilliance and dark.

Sergei then led us through the great Cathedral of the Assumption, Uspensky Sobor, modeled upon the cathedral of the same name in the Kremlin. Its blue, star-spangled domes are of incredible beauty and majesty. As Sergei and Alexander and I stepped out into the winter chill; the sky had turned a blue incredibly like that of the domes and, incredibly, star-spangled. The dusk deepened to the blue of the stained glass at Chartres. It was an evening like that on which I discovered, so unexpectedly, the little Church of the Trinity in the Sparrow Hills above Moscow twenty years before. It was a moment of transport, evanescent, nearly mystical.

Afterward, as we took our leave, I asked Father Iov a final question: "The monastery has existed for six hundred years. Will it be here in another six hundred years?" It was, I thought, even as I asked it, a fatuous question, and I was certain he would give me a positive answer. But he replied, "No, I do not think so." Father Iov explained that, in his view, there had been a severe decline of morality in Russia and in the world. Mankind had destroyed much of the earth, and was continuing to do so. Such a conviction, in that seat of holy faith, seemed remarkable to me. It seems less remarkable to me now that I reflect upon it. Father Iov's faith was not in this world, but elsewhere. I believed, and believe still, that the Trinity Monastery at Zagorsk will survive. I had seen the enduring spirit of Russia in the throngs of pilgrims, as I had in the Sparrow Hills twenty years before.

I came away from Zagorsk refreshed in my soul. I had come immediately into the presence of one of the wonders of the world. And in that venerable setting I had seen and heard in the faces and voices of the pilgrims the kind of faith and resolve that has survived generations of persecution and privation. I had sensed, as one must in this place, the enduring strength of the Russian spirit. Here was a point on the planet where survival and renewal are one.

I inventoried my memories on the night journey back to Moscow. Now and then I dozed, images of Chartres, of the Sparrow Hills, and of the splendors of the Trinity Monastery at Zagorsk, playing upon my eyelids. The little car chugged along into the labyrinth of Moscow, and then it broke down. After a short time another car mysteriously appeared and carried me off to dinner at the apartment of another old friend, Tatiana Kudriatseva, a translator and writer. The guests were lively and interesting people. The table was set with fine crystal and heavy silver, laden with dishes fit for a tsar. The wine and vodka were excellent; there were pâtés and cold cuts and fishes of remarkable character. "But where did you get this?" I asked. "Oh, it is available," she answered. "But it is unaffordable." Somehow she had managed. There was a bit of hope.

Tatiana's table was a far cry from the simple fare of Zagorsk, but it was in its own way a clear reflection also of an enduring Russia. There was a glitter like that I had seen in my dreams of country estates in the wooded reaches of Russia long ago, gleaming in snowy, moonlit meadows. When we raised a toast I could hear the bells of a troika in the delicate striking of the thinnest crystal.

On Bavarian Byways

Several years ago I was the house guest of a professor of American literature at the University of Würzburg, and it was my first time in Bavaria. Coming from a winter in Moscow, I was wholly alive to the sights and sounds of early summer in Western Europe. The Main River and the Franconian vineyards were scintillant in the sun, and the sky was blue. My host was a proper and hospitable man, and there was a free afternoon ahead of us. Would I care to see something of the countryside? Yes, indeed. Thereupon he produced a kind of concentrated library, an assortment of maps and guides and legends and photographs that closely defined the geography of the neighborhood.

After due deliberation, I said that I should very much like to see the cathedral at Bamberg. An excellent choice, my host exclaimed, and for the next hour, over Frankenwein coolers, we studied our subject as for an examination. Nothing was left to chance. I was greatly impressed. Here was the organized mind, here was discipline inspirational in itself. Afterward, on the autobahn, the professor drove with great efficiency, at speeds that seemed to measure risk in millimeters. And we missed the Bamberg exit. For the rest of the afternoon we traveled the back roads of the Steigerwald, looking for Bamberg. We arrived at the cathedral a few minutes after it had closed for the day.

As I think back on it, that excursion was not unfortunate, for I entered into the Bavarian landscape where its texture was whole and perceptible, unimpaired by ordinary and overworn routes of access. I happened into the deeper world. When such happenings occur, they ought to be thought of as blessings; they are the real enrichments of the journey.

The ordinary routes of access connect the great cities of the world, of course. If you venture through Bavaria from the north, as I did on that occasion, you will likely go more or less directly from Würzburg to Nuremberg to Munich. And in these principal cities you will miss much of the best that Bavaria has to offer.

It is the east of Bavaria that interests me here, for that area seems to me more engaging and less well known than other regions of the state. Let us say that I have a map of Bavaria and a drawing compass and I want to connect several towns and cities in such a way as to describe the arc or angle of Bavaria's eastern boundary. I begin at Bamberg, descend eastward to Regensburg, thence to Passau, which is the point of the angle, descend westward to Burghausen on the Salzach River, and lift my pencil from the map at Murnau on the Staffelsee, south and west of Munich. I have touched upon extraordinary places in my experience, places that exceed my expectations and in which for a time—a morning, a day, or a season—I was simply glad to be.

Eventually I did see the cathedral at Bamberg, a great thirteenth-century Romanesque building with four towers, and a basilica with three aisles. It is famous for its statues, especially the *Bamberger Reiter*, a striking figure of a young man on horseback. The attitude of the figure is graceful and serenely composed; ages in the rise to civilization coalesce in it. The rider is unmistakably noble in his manner. Everything about him bespeaks a quiet heroism. When I first saw the statue I wondered if it were not the very definition of the Teutonic ideal. I kept this in mind as I walked through the streets of the old city. And when I paused in a garden to slake my thirst with Rauchbier, the very distinctive "smoky beer" of Bamberg, I engaged a local citizen on the point. "Oh, that," he said. "*Bamberger Reiter!* Well, you put a man on a horse, and you see what happens. Poof!—right away you've got cowboys and Indians!"

By what seemed a remarkable coincidence, I found that same day the Karl May Museum in the Hainstrasse, a memorial to the writer who did so much to establish the American West in the modern European imagination and whose novels even now are familiar to virtually every German schoolboy and schoolgirl. Why yes, of course, I reflected, May's American Indian warrior, Winnetou, is noble too, and his lithe, stoic image is informed with quiet heroism. Cowboys and Indians indeed. Once I attended a Karl May Festival at Bad Segeberg, near Lübeck. It was a Wild West Show, Hanseatic style.

South and east of Bamberg, the woods and valleys succeed to the mists of the Bavarian Forest. Distance is a succession of blues.

The Nab and the Regen flow into the Danube at Regensburg. In this region the Danube is not blue but brown and gray and green. It is not as turbulent as the Inn or the Rhine, and it has a steady, almost tranquil appearance. But this appearance is misleading. The current of the Danube is swift and strong. If you place your demons in it, a saying goes, it will bear them all the way to the Black Sea, with time for lunch at Budapest.

There are cities in the world that are especially accessible to the imagination. You approach them and your blood runs faster; you enter them and you feel that you have kept an appointment of great moment, that you have been true to your destiny. Samarkand is such a city. Rome and Acoma are such cities. And Regensburg is one.

When you approach Regensburg—it matters not from which direction—your vision is drawn irresistibly to the spires of the *Dom*, St. Peter's Cathedral. They are visible for miles. With the exception of Chartres, I know of no other city that is so clearly dominated by its cathedral. They say that you cannot be lost in Regensburg—or even in the whole plain of the Danube—for there is always the magnificent, dark blue landmark of the *Dom* on the skyline.

The *Dom* is the darkest cathedral I have ever seen, inside and out, and its darkness is a thing to be pondered, for such darkness expresses the medieval intelligence more impressively than many architectural monuments. You behold this dark immensity and you know at some elemental level how it was that man thought of God at Regensburg in the thirteenth century.

The building is a textbook of the Gothic style, from early to late, and, as elsewhere in the city, there are fascinating juxtapositions. The *Eselturm* ("donkey tower"), for example, a tower from an earlier Romanesque building, is incorporated into the north side of the transept, and the effect is at once startling and complementary. You can dine in the courtyard of the Bischofshof below and contemplate this wonderful alliance well into the night.

The interior of the *Dom* is cold and cavernous, and though it is filled with unique works of art, it stands in sharp contrast to the density of gleaming and gilded interiors of the numerous Baroque churches for which Bavaria is famous. The word "austere" frequently attaches to such dark beauty as this, a quality that has inspired the great painters of Europe.

And this beauty can be nearly ineffable. One evening I came out of the Bischofshof and crossed the Residenzstrasse, my back to the cathedral. Suddenly, I became aware of an emphatic hush upon the scene. Everyone was looking up. I turned and caught my breath. The late light—it was well past eight o'clock in the middle of June—had struck fire to the *Dom*. But it was a fire such as I have never seen in stone, except once, deep in the heart of a crystal. The great dark limestone and sandstone blocks were green and glowing as if they had become vessels of strange, sulfurous light, not hard, but deeply luminous, as sometimes a fog is luminous in the dawn or dusk.

Fog swirls upon the Danube in the early morning and sometimes obscures the reach of the Steinerne Brücke, the old stone bridge that rivals the cathedral as the most venerable edifice in Regensburg. It was built in 1135-46 and was rightly regarded in the Middle Ages as a masterpiece of engineering, one of the wonders of the world. Its vaulted arches compress the Danube into churning eddies, making the upstream progress of river traffic, against the current, difficult at this point, and the fast downstream progress something of a challenge to a boatman. The Devil is said to hide in one of these arches. When the bridge and the cathedral were under construction, so the story goes, the two building masters entered into competition with each other to see which man could complete his job first. The *Brückenmeister* enlisted the aid of the Devil, offering him the first soul to cross the bridge. But when the bridge was finished, the clever man sent a dog across. So it was that the *Brückenmeister* won the competition and the Devil got only the soul of a poor dog.

If on a clear day you stand on the bridge and look south, you will have one of the very best views of the old city. Before you will be the ancient south tower of the bridge and next to it the *Salzstadel,* the old salt store, and just beyond will be the cathedral, like a great, majestic ship, floating above the pastel towers and the red roofs of Regensburg.

Below the high east face of the Salzstadel is the Historische Wurst-küche, the historic sausage kitchen. This tiny kitchen is said to be the oldest restaurant in Germany. It was officially established as a canteen for the bridge builders, and it has been in continuous use for eight hundred years; the great floods of the Danube are marked on its walls. In the winter you can sit inside at one of three tables in a neat and cozy room filled with the aroma of sizzling sausages and damn the cold. In the summer, when there are many more people to be served, you can sit outside under lofty umbrellas and gaze upon the Danube and the ancient bridge that spans it.

No one knows how old Regensburg is. Legend has it that it was founded by Norix, the son of Hercules. The region has been settled for six thousand years, and it contains archeological evidence of every culture since the Stone Age. In pre-Christian times there was a Celtic settlement on this site called Ratisbon or Ratisbona. (Regensburg still bears this ancient name on modern maps in France and Italy.) In A.D. 179, under the command of the Emperor Marcus Aurelius, the Romans completed the military fortress of Castra Regina, "Camp on the Regen," head-quarters of the supreme military commander of the province of Raetia. Massive Roman walls are still very much in evidence in Regensburg; they have for almost two thousand years determined the boundaries of the city center. One of the entrances to the Bischofshof is a splendid Roman arch, the Porta Praetoria. In 1873 workmen excavated a stone inscription, some ten feet in length, that was made to commemorate the completion of Castra Regina. This imposing record of the founding of Regensburg is unique among the cities of Germany.

But Regensburg is preeminently a medieval city, perhaps the most authentic and best preserved medieval city in the country. The citizens of Regensburg are keenly aware of their city and of its riches, but they bear their good fortune easily and well. In no sense do they think of themselves as the inhabitants of a museum. They live comfortably in their thirteenth-century houses; they attend concerts in their dark cathedral, and they ride modern buses across their old stone bridge.

There is a great satisfaction in walking through the streets of a medieval city. For a time I lived in Regensburg, in the Gravenreuther House, named for Konrad Gravenreuther, who owned the building in 1381. Now owned by the University of Regensburg, it stands in the Hinter der Grieb, a short, narrow street that is especially characteristic of medieval Regensburg. The house is a marvelous structure, with groups of early Gothic windows in the facade and an oriel-like bay window. There I lived through one summer. Regensburg is far enough north (it lies on or near the same latitude as Winnipeg, Canada) to have long, luminous summer evenings. Countless times I ventured out upon the town in the low light. Most often I walked to the east end of Hinter der Grieb and through the courtyard of the Goldener Turm, a magnificent nine-story patrician tower of the thirteenth century that once had the distinction of being the tallest building north of the Alps, across Wahlenstrasse and into Kramgasse, one of the streets I like best in the world. It is very narrow and cobbled, with many crooks in it. There are shops and cafes all along, and there is also the Blomberg House, where lived Barbara Blomberg, a woman about whom I know little but have often dreamed; there, in 1547, after a liaison with Emperor Charles V, she gave birth to the future Don John of Austria. At certain points in the Kramgasse you can look to the end and see framed there the north tower and spire of the *Dom*. It is a sight not to be forgotten.

The country surrounding Regensburg is undulant. There are woods and farms—and woodpiles in the country villages. "Piles" is not an accurate word here. Firewood is stacked or placed or fitted into geometries in Bavaria. These constructions are rustic works of art.

Near Regensburg is the gorge of the Danube and Kloster Weltenburg, the oldest abbey in Bavaria. Its Baroque chapel is the work of the famous brothers Asam. On the high altar is a magnificent gilded statue of St. George. A cave in the adjacent Altmuhl Valley contains paintings that date from 15,000 B.C. There are also several notable castles in the valley. Randeck Castle, near Essing, seems held in suspension above huge pinnacles of Jurassic rock, and a little to the north and west is Prunn Castle, known as the jewel of the Altmuhl Valley.

The Danube flows southeast from Regensburg, tracing the lower edge of the Bavarian Forest, to Passau, where it is joined by the Inn and the Ilz. There is often haze on the forest, which softens the horizon and holds it away. In Passau snapdragons grow out of the old city walls. You find yourself in a labyrinth of alleys, with great curving walls leaning over you, blind corners everywhere and quaint little flying buttresses that, you imagine, hold the city up. Then suddenly you emerge in bright, open space, under a blue sky, in view of one river or another. Or you step out into the Domplatz, with its flower and vegetable markets, your gaze fixed upon the high cupolas of St. Stephen's Cathedral. The interior is Baroque and filled with light, so different from St. Peter's of Regensburg. Standing in the center aisle you are struck by three things; the crisp modernity of the high altar with its depiction, by the Munich sculptor Joseph Henselmann, of the stoning of Saint Stephen, the brilliance of the gilt pulpit, a superb eighteenth-century work, and the organ, the largest church organ in the world, with its five manuals, 231 stops, and 17,463 pipes.

Passau has a kind of international character that you do not find elsewhere in Bavaria. The work "international" suggests a quality of sophistication, I suppose, but that is not what I mean. Passau is not as sophisticated as Munich, say, or Nuremberg, but it is international in its history, in its idea of itself. There is a centuries-old rivalry between Passau and Salzburg for political and ecclesiastical eminence. Italian influences have marked not only the style of architecture in Passau but also its way of life. Then, of course, Eastern Europe is next door. There are many confluences, it seems. This is Bohemian Bavaria.

To the south, along a wide bend of the Inn, there is an extensive plain. The haze disappears and the sky expands. Here and there the landscape has about it the reach of the American plains. At Braunau, the Salzach Valley opens to the south.

The castle at Burghausen stands on a long, high spit of land above the Salzach River and Worhsee. Burghausen Castle is first mentioned in a document dated 1025 as being a royal court, though it seems likely to have been a *Pfaiz* (imperial palace) of the Bavarian dukes as early as the seventh century. The present castle was completed in 1490. Many parts of the earliest courtyard, however, date from 1255. The castle complex, six courtyards or baileys, extends for 1,200 yards from the entrance at the sixth courtyard to the point of the spit. Each of the baileys was constructed in a different period, so that, walking the length of the castle, you have an uncanny sense of walking through time.

When I came to Burghausen, I had ceased to believe in castles. I had seen many of the castles of Europe, more perhaps than I could assimilate in my mind; they were either magnificent ruins, or they were medieval shells in which were enclosed musty museums or modern hotels. But as I was sketching the oldest courtyard at Burghausen, my imagination hovering in that intricate space among narrow windows and long stairways and numberless arches, at crude angles and rings of iron, along terraces reaching down and planes ascending, my deepest belief in castles was restored. This is a world in itself, I thought. If I lived here, I would not easily know the need to be elsewhere; my life would be full. You do not perceive Burghausen through a glass—the clearest glass of a showcase will distort a truth on the other side. But this is Burghausen, and here is nothing false, nothing that imitates itself. This is a real castle.

The lower end of my hypothetical angle runs down and crosses, then parallels, the Inn just north of the Austrian border. It ends at the village of Murnau. Historically, Murnau's importance is modest. It boasts no great architectural monuments, no roots into antiquity, no time remembered of glory. But it is remarkably beautiful and remarkably Bavarian, and I would have it here for its own sake.

A comprehensive photograph of Murnau would be composed of cows in the foreground, the village beyond, an end of the Staffelsee in the middle distance, then woods and the snow-covered Alpenvorland in the background—green ascending to blue. But better than this hypothetical photograph are the paintings of Murnau in the manner of the Blue Rider school that hang at the Lenbach Gallery in Munich—Gabriele Munter's *View of the Murnau Moor*, for example, or Alexei von Jawlensky's

Summer Evening in Murnau, both painted in 1908. These are brilliant distillations of the Bavarian landscape.

I have been to Murnau only once, but it remains in my mind's eye, a vivid and immediate presence. I took the train down from Munich, an hour's ride. A friend had told me that I should have a look at the Munter house there. It was a fine day for walking, and I took my time moving though the village streets, pausing frequently to look into shop windows and gardens. The air, the same air that had touched the Staffelsee and the Alpine foothills, was delicious and fragrant with lilacs. At length I met an old gentleman and his wife. *"Grüssgott!"* we greeted each other. *"Wo ist das Munter-Haus, bitte?"* The old man saw at once that I was insecure in my German, and he became at once generous in his spirit. He took me very firmly by the arm, turned me halfway around, and pointed. "Yellow house," he said with emphasis, and his wife bore him out. "Yellow house," she said. And there, across a green depression full of wildflowers, was the very house I had seen in a Munter painting entitled *The Russians' House* in the Lenbach Gallery a year before. There, at Kottmullerallee 6, Gabriele Munter had lived with Wassily Kandinsky from 1908 to 1914; and after a time away she returned there to live out her life. It is a beautiful house. In the atelier are the palettes and brushes of the two artists, furniture they decorated, and reproductions of some of their paintings. The views from the atelier windows of the village and the moors and foothills of the Alps are nearly perfect.

I returned to Munich that same afternoon, and the next day I revisited the Lenbach Gallery, there to sit for a time among the paintings of Murnau. They confirmed me in my vision of a new prospect, wide and deep. The angle I drew on the verge of eastern Bavaria is well completed in this museum here in the south, reflected among its bright pigments, distilled in the alembic of the painter's eye.

Granada: A Vision of the Unforeseen

"Pomegranate," the lady said.

It was blustery in the late winter, and I was approaching Granada from the north, down the spine of the country. I had never been in Andalusia, and my anticipation was high. The strains of *Boléro* had wafted in my brain for days. In my mind's eye was a sunlit city on a hill, a city of gleaming white walls and red tiles, and beyond, a snow-capped range of mountains against a deep blue sky. And in the middle distance, on another hill, between the city and the mountains, was a great red castle of incomparable beauty and majesty. This was, of course, the *Calat-alhamra* of the Moorish kings of Spain, the Alhambra. I had done some homework.

In Madrid, on the eve of my arrival in Granada, the crowds were heavy in the shopping streets, and the shop windows blazed. In Spain, people come alive at night; it is an axiom that they sleep less than other people. I dined with a small party at the Ritz Hotel. My companions were all natives of Spain, well traveled, and they were concerned to welcome and assist me. The conversation came down to me and my destination. "I am going to Granada," I said. "Pomegranate," the lady on my left said. "Granada is the Spanish word for pomegranate."

The next afternoon I crossed the rivers of the south, the Tagus, the Guadiana, and the Guadalquivir, pausing overnight at the Parador de Toledo, from the terrace of which the view of the old Roman city is remarkable at any time of the day or night. Especially in the low light of the late afternoon does Toledo become, like the pueblos of the American Southwest, a city of gold.

On the vast tableland of Castille-La Mancha there are abandoned haciendas in the foreground, and castle ruins on the skyline. There is a hint of desolation and an unforgiving aspect to this land, a resonance of the Extremadura next door to the west, from which came so many of the Conquistadores, men peculiarly equal to the hardships of the New World. (Perhaps they bore seeds as well as swords. Along Coronado's route in Mexico and Arizona I have seen hummingbirds at a hundred pomegranate trees.)

In Andalusia, in the vicinity of the town of Jaen, the land rolled beneath bare, brooding mountains so sharply defined as to seem cut out of paper. There were endless groves of olives in intricate patchworks as far as the eye could see. Here, in 1246, when the Castilians were encroaching upon other Almoravid states of al-Andalus, an Arab chieftain, Mohammed ibn-Yusuf ibn-Nasr, moved his capital to the south, to the town of Karnattah, where he established the Nasrid dynasty. Granada (the name, and by coincidence the Spanish word for pomegranate, is a corruption of the Arab *Karnattah*) flourished in the thirteenth and fourteenth centuries. It became the last bastion of Arabic–Andaluz art and architecture in all of Iberia. And of this great artistic enterprise, the fortress-palace complex of the Alhambra is the supreme example.

The obsession of Queen Isabella's reign was the Reconquista, the subjugation of the Moors and the return of all Spain to Catholicism. In 1484 she sent King Ferdinand into the field to accomplish her purpose, and he did so in just eight years. The final scenes were played out at Granada. Boabdil el Chico, son of Abu al-Hassan, king of Karnattah, came to the throne in 1482. Ferdinand captured him twice and made him a puppet of the Castilians. Having renounced the throne, Boabdil changed his mind and decided to fight for what remained of the Moorish kingdom. Ferdinand placed the city under siege. Two years later Boabdil agreed to surrender. On January 2, 1492, the Reconquista was complete. Religious toleration, however, remained in effect until Cardinal Cisneros arrived in 1499, determined to rid Spain of the last remnants of Moorish culture. Between 1609 and 1614, the last Muslims were turned out, even those who had converted to Christianity.

This is a sad story, and a kind of sadness underlies the beauty of Granada, a delicate but pervasive melancholy. The famous *granadino* Federico García Lorca wrote that he remembered Granada "as one should remember a sweetheart who has died." It is said that there are old families in Morocco who still hold with longing the keys to their former homes in Granada.

I arrived in the late afternoon, and it was no longer winter. Everywhere was color. The air was warm and delicious after rain. The city, from virtually every point of view, is singular and stately. It seems almost meticulous in its design, cohesive, concentrated, integral. Many cities of our time sprawl beyond the plane of their composition. Granada, despite its population of 288,000, does not. Nor can I think of another city of which the natural setting is more complementary. On a clear morning the sky is an exquisite blue, the trees, which seem intrinsic, are of a deep, scintillant green, and on the southern horizon is the long, snow-capped Sierra Nevada range. The city, the great plain from which it rises, and the mountains are a definition of inland Andalusia.

Granada is built on three hills, the Albaicin, the Sacromonte, and the Alhambra. On the first of these the Moors built their first fortress, then their splendid white town houses with their luxuriant gardens behind long white walls. The Albaicin, on the right bank of the Darro, is dominated by the Gothic church of San Nicolas. From this point, in the late afternoon, one has an extraordinary view of the Alhambra across the river. There is no Granada, no Andalusia, no Spain without the red-orange walls of the Alhambra.

The Sacromonte, also on the right bank of the Darro, is opposite the Alhambra and the Generalife, or summer palace of the rulers of Granada. The hillside is marked by a network of paths that lead to Gypsy caves. Some of the caves are elaborate in their decoration and craftwork. Here at night the Gypsies sing and dance for the entertainment of tourists, and they have a well-earned reputation for hard-selling everything from carnations to the telling of fortunes. An old, toothless man, dressed elegantly (if you did not look too close) in black insisted on dancing a flamenco for me alone, he said—"*para usted, solo, señor.*" The dance was a parody, a delicate and precarious performance; it spoke of the melancholy of the clown.

I stayed in the Parador de San Francisco, on the Alhambra hill, in the Alhambra complex itself. This small, elegant, and expensive establishment is perhaps the most famous of all *paradors*. It is part of the old Convent of San Francisco, built in the fifteenth century, where Ferdinand and Isabella were interred in its church until the royal mausoleums were completed in the Capilla Real in the lower town. The Parador is richly appointed, comfortable, and altogether compatible with the great fortress-palace of which it is a part. It is surrounded by magnificent gardens, and it offers prime views of the grounds below, the city, and the countryside beyond. On my first evening there, I dined downstairs in the dining room, and I enjoyed a dish that is unique to Granada, the famous *tortilla al Sacromonte*; this is an omelet cooked in the Sacromonte Gypsy manner, with a filling of brains, lamb's testicles, and vegetables. My good wine bore the name Sangre del Toro.

The next morning I began my tour of the Alhambra. I stood before the palace of Charles V, who was elected Holy Roman Emperor in 1520. Designed in 1526 by Pedro Machuca, who studied under Michelangelo, and considered an excellent example of Spanish Renaissance art, it is a massive, square building in the classical style, of an elegance conspicuously unlike that of the Nasrid Palace next door. Indeed, it seems in clear opposition to the Moorish style that predominates here until you realize that opposition and contrast are informing principles of the Alhambra. The red castle is a definition of elegance, and a repository of some of the most delicate and intricate art in the world on the one hand, and it is a monolithic, seemingly impenetrable, fortress on the other.

The palace is, in any case, a fitting monument to Charles V, whose reign inaugurated Spain's golden age and whose empire extended over most of western Europe. Certainly it reflects the considerable power he wielded and the tenacity with which he held on to his inheritances. The palace is a precise circle within the courtyard, a precise square. Bullfights once took place inside.

The Alcazaba, at the west end, is the oldest, pre-Nasrid part of the Alhambra, dating back to the ninth century. From the Torre de la Vela, you can look down upon the whole of the city, across the length of the palace grounds to the Sacromonte, the Generalife, and all the way to the blue mountains on the circle of the sky.

I proceeded to the Nasrid Palace. This complex, which is the heart of the Alhambra, was constructed around the Myrtle and Lion Courts in the fourteenth century. It includes, among its architectural riches, the Mexuar Court, the Hall of the Ambassadors, the Abencerrajes Gallery, the King's Chamber, and the Daraxa Mirador. The Mexuar was a seat of judicial administration. In it there is a marvelous carved wooden cornice and many kinds of tile and stucco decoration. The Hall of the Ambassadors, often called the jewel of the Alhambra, was the audience chamber of the emirs. It has a magnificent domed ceiling made of cedarwood with intricate carvings, a tiled floor, inscriptions from the Koran and other texts in stuccowork, and bay windows which offer views of the city and the plain, or *vega*. The Abencerrajes Gallery has superbly decorated arches, slender columns, magnificent tilework, a stalactite ceiling, a star-shaped cupola, and a central basin. It was in this basin that Boabdil placed the severed heads of thirty-six of his subjects suspected of treason. The King's Chamber is a row of alcoves on the vaulting of which are painted scenes of Moorish and Christian princes at leisure, a mysterious departure from the general decoration. The Daraxa Mirador overlooks the Daraxa Garden. The garden itself is luxuriant with trees and flowers and the fragrance of oranges and spice. The centerpiece of the Myrtle Court is a long, narrow reflecting pool, banked by hedges of myrtle and stocked with large goldfishes. The Court of Lions contains a low, large white marble fountain, ringed by twelve stone lions. The loveliness of the surrounding arches, supported by numerous, slender columns, is serene. The lions are not quite crude, but softly defined, pleasing and preposterous. Utterly without ferocity, they bear a likeness to English sheepdogs in a state of languor and satiety. And in the rich gardens around there are narrow canals of running, rippling water. And there are cats, more formidable than the stone lions, innumerable and ubiquitous. The cats of the Alhambra are now its rightful residents. And there are pomegranates.

There are two Alhambras, at least: one to know by day and one to know by night. (One of the real benefits of staying in the Parador de San Francisco is that you can wander in and around the Alhambra at night, when the complex is not open to the public.) In the night the palace becomes softly luminous. The great towers shine low, and loom and impend upon the shadows. The moon touches magic to all the facets and seams and grooves and angels. A thousand intricate shapes shimmer in pools. The soft light pours upon the courtyards and filters through the lacework to effect kaleidoscopic patterns on patterns. In the Hall of the Ambassadors the tiled floor, which seemed colorless in the day, is carpeted with deep and delicate hues. The gardens are paradisal in the moonlight. There emanates from the Alhambra at night an ethereal radiation like the aura of stars.

To be sure, there is more to Granada than the Alhambra. The Capilla Real, begun in 1506 and completed in 1521, is a unique equation of design and decoration, which houses an impressive collection of art objects. It is of a grandeur befitting the Catholic monarchs, who wanted to be buried on the site of their ultimate victory over the Moors.

The Cartuja is a majestic complex in the Baroque style. The sacristy, especially, is impressive in its stuccowork, marble molding, and its cedarwood furniture inlaid with the most colorful metals, tortoise shells, and mother of pearl. It has been called the Christian Alhambra.

But the work that is the Alhambra itself is a wonder of the world. The highest expression of Muslim art left to us, it is made of exquisite webs and tracery, fragile filigree, meticulous calligraphy, tilework of the purest symmetry, and finally some profound and mysterious notion of beauty in the human brain, extending to creation at the human hand. It is a thing to seek out and behold with wonder.

New Mexico: Passage into Legend

When I have gone traipsing after legends I have been a happy man. In Central Asia I have covered ground upon which Tamerlane and Alexander the Great walked. I have meandered, as did Julius Caesar, through the forums of Rome. Like Rasmussen I have known the dogs of Thule. I have followed upon the trail of Lewis and Clark, ventured after Custer and Crazy Horse in the Black Hills, and traced the migration route of my Kiowa ancestors down the rain shadow of the Rocky Mountains from the Yellowstone to the Washita. In dreams I read my mythic maps.

And from my travels I return to the Southwest, to New Mexico. La Tierra del Encanto has for me the gravity of the moon. Even when I look across the world, it is the canyon country of my boyhood that I see. There, among cowboys and Indians, is an enchantment that comprehends the richness and variety of the continent itself. To be for a time in the long valleys of the Rio Grande or the Pecos or in the foothills of the Jemez or the Sangre de Cristo Mountains, or in the sandy reaches of the borderlands below the Butterfield Trail, is to bear the mind and heart into a particular space, an immensity of earth and sky that, for want of a better term, we call the Wild West. But, no, I take that back. There is no better term. The Wild West signifies a geography and a time in our experience that defines the American imagination.

I come for to sing:

> Come down, Billy, to Lincoln town;
> come down, you kid of great renown.

All right, Patrick, I'll come with you,
and then, pray tell, what will we do?
We'll dance a jig and dine on shoat,
and you shall be my billy goat.

Lincoln, New Mexico, lies in the southeast quadrant of the state, a sleepy village nestled beside the Rio Bonito, in the foothills of the Capitan Mountains. The country is high—Lincoln itself is nearly six thousand feet above sea level—and verdant: ranch county. The sky is the blue of the sky farther north, the sky at Abiquiu, say, or at Tierra Amarilla. It is a blue that artists love, deep and sheer and vibrant. On a clear day the early morning light is pure and glinting of a brightness that informs the sands and leaves and streams with brilliance. In the late afternoon there is a golden depth to the earth, a low smoldering of the setting sun.

Time touches Lincoln very lightly. Its one and only street is lined with old trees and old houses, mostly adobe, clean and well cared for. But it is worth remembering that in nine years, from 1872 to 1881, forty-three people died violent deaths on that mile-long stretch. Most of the dead were casualties of the infamous Lincoln County war, arguably the most violent chapter in the history of the Wild West.

In 1875, Lincoln numbered some four hundred inhabitants. Among them were two retired army officers, L. G. Murphy and J. J. Dolan, who established a merchandising empire: they sold supplies to nearby Fort Stanton, and they were the only outfitters to the farmers and ranchers of the neighborhood. Then a young Englishman, John Tunstall, came to Lincoln to set up a competing business and enlisted the help of an attorney, Alexander McSween, to promote his enterprise. Since Murphy and Dolan controlled the law in Lincoln County, Tunstall formed a band, the "Regulators," for protection. One of them, in whom Tunstall inspired an intense loyalty, was Henry McCarty, alias William H. Bonney, alias Kid Antrim, alias Billy the Kid.

The war began in earnest following Tunstall's murder in February 1878. Its climactic moment came during a five-day battle the following

July in which the Murphy-Dolan forces laid siege to the McSween house, where Billy and others were holed up. As the house burned to the ground, Billy escaped; Alexander McSween was killed on the spot.

In today's Lincoln, there is a vacant lot where the McSween house was. The Tunstall store still stands near the middle of the town. At the western end of the street, opposite the Wortley Hotel, is the courthouse. It was from this courthouse that Billy the Kid escaped on April 29, 1881, having shot and killed his captors, J. W. Bell and Robert Olinger.

Lincoln is the center of my pilgrimage, but it is the middle mile, as it were, in a journey through some of the most beautiful and powerful geography in the Southwest, a land of enchantment indeed, and a legendary way. It is also a journey that weaves into story the last hundred days of Henry McCarty's life.

If you place a ruler diagonally on the lower half of a map of New Mexico and draw a straight line from La Mesilla, on the lower Rio Grande, to Fort Summer, on the Pecos, your line will extend northeastward across the Organ Mountains to the White Sands National Monument, through the Mescalero Apache Reservation, through Ruidoso, San Patricio and Lincoln, and across the vast plain of the Pecos to Fort Summer and the Bosque Redondo.

La Mesilla, just south of the city of Las Cruces, is an old settlement of particular character. The first European to see the Mesilla Valley was Alvar Nunuz Cabeza de Baca, who, having been shipwrecked, walked across the present states of Louisiana and Texas in search of Spanish settlements. He arrived here in 1535. The church of San Albino, dominant in the clean geometry of mission architecture, was built on the La Mesilla plaza in 1850. In La Mesilla the Gadsden Treaty was signed in 1854, creating the present boundary between the United States and Mexico. La Posta, now a popular restaurant, was a station on the Butterfield stage line that ran from St. Louis to Los Angeles, the only one still standing. On April 13, 1881, in a building that still stands on the La Mesilla plaza across the narrow street from La Posta, Billy the Kid, having been convicted of murder in the Lincoln County War, was sentenced to be hanged at Lincoln on May 13, 1881. On April 13 he began his last ride, as it was thought to be, his arms and legs in chains in an ambulance. It must have been a strange, wakeful journey. It lasted five days. Among his seven guards were his deadly enemies Billy Mathews, who had shot him in the leg in 1878, and Robert Olinger, who was to die at his hands within the fortnight.

Legendstalker, I set out on the same trail. At five o'clock in the afternoon I am in the foothills of the Organ Mountains. Their great pinnacles ride in the blue infinity, among rolling, billowing clouds full of light. The towering pipes are bare rock, gray and impending. They rise vertically out of steep green and rust slopes. The heat is heavy. This is wild, bristling country, cactus- and rock-ridden. There is only one other human in sight, a man far away across the spiny growth. We greet each other with a wave of our hats. I am carrying a liter of warm water. I wonder if Billy the Kid's hunger and thirst were relieved in the ambulance. I imagine Mathews and Olinger passing tortillas and a bottle of whiskey back and forth to each other.

San Augustin Pass is a vantage point that seems to draw the whole planet to the eye. On the north, the San Andres Mountains curve out into the Malpais. On the south, like a tremendous wave, is the wall of the Organs, its ragged ridge running down to El Paso del Norte. To the west are the Mesilla Valley and the Jornada del Muerto, a long, unforgiving stretch on the trail from Chihuahua to Santa Fe, named for its heat and desolation. And to the east the Tularosa Basin and the White Sands, a plain extending as far as the eye can see. There are places where the earth concentrates its strength; this is one of them. The wind whips my sleeves and raddles my hair. My eyes burn and tear in the hard, dry light. Something of the night's cold already wells in the shadows along the ridge. I sense that I am at the confluence of many powers running, rolling, soaring, wheeling, sweeping. I continue along the ruler's edge, descending, leveling off, ascending.

The Mescalero Apache Reservation lies on both the east and west slopes of the Sacramento Range. Its 460,000 acres of heavily forested land are dominated by Sierra Blanca, at 12,003 feet the highest peak in southern New Mexico. In its shadow is an incomparable landscape, one that is anomalously wild and luxurious. Here, at 7,200 feet, is the Inn of the Mountain Gods, one of the principal all-seasons resorts in the

Southwest. Owned by the Mescalero Apache tribe, the Inn, at once rustic and modern, is set on a pristine lake that provides the guest with fishing, sailing, and canoeing.

As a child, I came into these mountains with my father to hunt turkey. I have heard the cold, clear water running fast in the mountain streams, and I have seen the Apache *ga'an* dancers in the firelight. In those days I could not have dreamed of a multicourse dinner in the Dan Li Ka Restaurant amid elegance such as this. But in the morning, when I go out into the chill, fresh mountain air and see the snow glistening on Sierra Blanca, I can see the world as it was in the 1940s, as it was in Henry McCarty's day, and as it has been from the beginning of time.

Billy the Kid knew little enough of luxury, but he knew the Mescalero Apache Reservation. It was established by executive order of President Ulysses S. Grant on May 27, 1873, the year Billy witnessed his mother's marriage to William H. Antrim in Santa Fe. On the reservation is the ruin of Blazer's Sawmill, where Billy the Kid and other Regulators fought a curious battle against one Andrew L. "Buckshot" Roberts on April 4, 1878. Mortally wounded early in the fight, Roberts barricaded himself in the mill owner's office, and with J. H. Blazer's .45-60 hunting rifle held off the Regulators through a long, hot day. Several of the Regulators were wounded, and Roberts managed to kill Dick Brewer, their captain. Brewer and Roberts were buried side by side in an obscure cemetery on a rise above the walls of the old mill. Although the graves are now well marked, it is reputedly not known which man is in which grave.

One of Billy the Kid's favorite places was San Patricio, a village north of the Mescalero Reservation and a few miles below Lincoln which was established by Irish soldiers mustered out of the army in 1866. The Church of St. Patrick was built in the 1870s.

Remarkably, San Patricio is now distinguished by notable art galleries and two polo fields. The San Patricio gallery of John Meigs is a fascinating hodgepodge of paintings, prints, books, and what have you.

The Hurd-La Rinconada Gallery is a handsome adobe structure adjacent to a polo field on the historic Sentinel Ranch. The artist Peter Hurd became interested in polo while a student at the New Mexico

Military Institute at Roswell. The field is used regularly by teams from Mexico and the United States; the gallery shows original works by Peter Hurd, Henrietta Wyeth, Michael Hurd, Andrew Wyeth, and N. C. Wyeth.

San Patricio, a name that is an Irish–Native New Mexican equation, must have appealed to Billy the Kid, to the McCarty and El Chivato in him. He was always looking for a home.

In the afternoon I am hard upon the legend. I am sitting over coffee and a peach cobbler in the Wortley Hotel in Lincoln, New Mexico, on the most dangerous street in America. Hope, the daughter of the proprietor, approaches me, and we make friends. She is remarkably pretty and gracious, and yesterday was her sixth birthday.

"What do you do in real life?" I ask her.

"I'm a writer," she replies.

"Hope, I believe that you are the very person I'm looking for," I say. "The big house across the street, the courthouse, do you know about it?"

"Oh, yes, my friend Jack is there. Come, I'll show it to you." She takes me by the hand.

"Wait. Did you hear a shot?"

"What?"

"Never mind." I had heard a shot, I was sure. Pat Garrett, Sheriff of Lincoln County, had gone to White Oaks to get lumber for the scaffold on which Billy would be hanged on Friday the 13th of May. There were only two people in the courthouse, as far as I knew, Billy the Kid and J. W. Bell, who guarded him.

Hope leads me in Bob Olinger's very tracks. Bell is dead. As we come to the corner of the courthouse I know that if I look up I shall see in the open window Billy's familiar face, and I shall see into the twin barrels of Olinger's Whitneyville shotgun. It was with Olinger's own gun, his signature, that Billy killed him.

Inside "The House," as it came to be known early on (it was built as the home of L. G. Murphy & Company), Hope introduces me to Jack Rigney, the ranger in charge of the Lincoln State Monument. The courthouse is big, with dark rooms and bright rooms. There are two floors, each an area of 2,800 square feet; the ceilings are eleven feet high. The floors are connected by a single stairway inside and a double stairway joined by a balcony outside. Jack is generous, patient. He answers my questions, volunteers critical information, gives me all the time I want to myself. I climb the stairs, the seventeen steps, slowly, imagining the two men upon them in April 1881. On one of these steps a bullet from Billy's gun passed through Bell's body and killed him. The bullet hole in the wall at the foot of the stair is still there. I am taking the same way Billy took to the corner window of the room in which he was incarcerated, indeed chained at night to a bolt in the floor. Here, or there, he finds the Whitneyville and takes it to the window. And then I am standing exactly where he stood, and the barrels gleam under my aim, and Olinger is looking up at me. It is a terrible moment, of such tension that I shake.

Hope is sitting on the top of the stairs. "Do you know what happened here?" I asked her. She nods, but I don't know what her nod means. The next evening I will see her and her mother at the Tinnie Silver Dollar Restaurant at nearby Tinnie, New Mexico. She will be wearing a white fiesta dress, and she and I will exchange pleasantries, and I shall again be enchanted. Hope, Girl of the Golden West.

Again in the dangerous street I see Billy taking his leave. He shakes hands with the townspeople, and on a borrowed horse he rides away out of sight. Between here and there he passes into legend.

My mind snaps back into history. From that day Billy the Kid had less han three months to live, and he lived on the run. He had many friends in the territory, and they took care of him. His closest friends, those who most resembled a family, were in and around Fort Sumner. In his last days he stayed with sheepherders in their camps and stole into Fort Sumner to dance with pretty women.

Old Fort Sumner is gone. There are only historical markers, a few reconstructed walls, a museum and the little cemetery in which Billy the Kid and a few others lie buried. It is a somber place, a place for pilgrimage, a place for muted wonder and meditation. And it is a sacred place, consecrated with blood and sacrifice.

In the early 1860s the Navajos and the Apaches resisted the relentless intrusion into their homelands. The United States Army then set about removing them from their land and placing them in captivity. Under the command of Colonel Christopher "Kit" Carson, federal troops raided the Mescalero Apache tribe. Nearly five hundred captives were marched to the Bosque Redondo, the site of Fort Sumner. In the winter of 1863-64, Carson raided and pillaged the Navajos, starving them into submission. They were then forced to make the Long Walk, a distance of some three hundred miles to the Bosque Redondo. In the fall of 1864 there were nearly ten thousand Indians, Apaches, and Navajos on the Bosque Redondo Reservation.

The reservation "solution" was a dismal failure. Drought, hail, and cutworms destroyed crops. Irrigation from the Pecos River so burdened the soil with salt that it became infertile. Homesickness and the devastation of morale took a terrible toll. One night in 1865 the Apaches escaped en masse in what is surely one of the truly remarkable military actions in our history. In 1868 the Navajos were allowed to return to their homeland.

Fort Sumner was then abandoned by the military, and the former reservation was purchased by Lucien Maxwell, a cattleman whose land holdings totaled more than two million acres. Maxwell converted one of the officers' quarters into a large family residence. In 1881 the house was overseen by his son Pete. The old fort had become a lively village.

In the middle of the night, on July 14, 1881, Pat Garrett came with two deputies to the Maxwell house. Leaving his deputies outside on the porch, Garrett entered Pete Maxwell's bedroom. The two men talked in the dark. Garrett was hunting Billy the Kid. Suddenly a figure entered upon the porch, startled the two men there, and ducked into the bedroom. Billy had come, half dressed, to cut a piece of meat from a side of beef that had been butchered that day and hung from the roof of the porch. He carried a knife in one hand and a pistol in the other. Alarmed, he spoke the words *"Quien es?"*—Who is it?—to Pete Maxwell. In that moment he unaccountably, fatally, hesitated. Recognizing the voice, Pat Garrett drew his pistol and fired twice. The first shot killed Billy the Kid. The second slammed into the headboard of the bed.

A candle was placed in the window. The Maxwell women grieved, and there was wailing in the town. Henry McCarty is generally believed to have been twenty-one years old at the time of this death.

Standing on the edge of the reconstruction, looking into the recess where the Maxwell house stood, then just later at the gravestone, I hear not a dirge but soft, distant sounds of revelry, the music of a baile, laughter, the contented voices of the dead under the rustle of orchard leaves.

The Homestead on Rainy Mountain Creek

The house and arbor stand on a rise on the plain east of the town of Mountain View. A little to the north and west are the Washita River and Rainy Mountain Creek. A few miles to the south and west is Rainy Mountain itself, scarcely a mountain, rather a knoll or a hummock. But in a way it is a singular feature in the immediate landscape. From the top of Rainy Mountain you can see a long way in any direction. It is said that when the Kiowas camped on this ground, it inevitably rained, thus the name. At the base of the mountain is the ruin of the old Rainy Mountain School, which my grandmother, Aho, attended as a young girl. Nearby is the Rainy Mountain Baptist Church and the cemetery in which many of my forebears are buried.

The house was built in 1913, the year my father was born. He was in fact born while the house was under construction, in a tepee close to where the arbor now stands, on the corner closest to the well. And in that house and arbor he grew up with his sister, Clara, and his brothers, James, Lester, and Ralph.

My grandfather, Mammedaty, was greatly respected by all who knew him. For one thing, he was a successful farmer. The Kiowas, who migrated to the southern plains from the north, were a nomadic tribe of hunters; they never had an agrarian tradition. In my grandfather's day, when only a generation before the old roving life of the buffalo hunter had been intact, the Kiowas did not take easily to farming. Their land was fertile, but they preferred to lease it to white farmers. Mammedaty was an exception. He worked hard, and he saw that his sons worked hard. He made a good life for himself and his family.

I never knew my grandfather. He died in 1933, the year before I was born. But I feel I knew him. His powerful presence was discernible in his wife and children, in the homestead on Rainy Mountain Creek, and in the countless stories I was told about him. All my life he has been an inspiration to me. His grandfather was the great chief Lone Wolf, and his grandmother was Kau-au-ointy, a Mexican captive who raised a great herd of cattle and became a prominent figure in the tribe. His mother, Keahdinekkeah, loved him above all others, I am told, and when he died she had him buried in a bronze casket, over which she placed her favorite shawl.

My grandmother, Aho, was the principal force in the homestead when I was a child. She was a beautiful and gracious woman, and she presided over family affairs with great generosity and goodwill. She was in her middle fifties when I was born, and she died at the age of eighty-five. About the time of her death I was writing *The Way to Rainy Mountain*, and in that writing I retraced the migration route of the Kiowas from western Montana to Oklahoma. My pilgrimage ended at my grand-mother's grave. The introduction to *The Way to Rainy Mountain* is in large measure an evocation of my grandmother's spirit, and for this reason among others that book is my favorite of my works.

The house seems small to me now, but when I was a child it was grand and full of life. Aho and my uncle Jimmy, who never married, were always there. There were frequent reunions when my aunt Clara and my other uncles, Lester and Ralph, my cousins, and my parents and I convened to rejoice in the institution of our family. There were fre-quent visitors, kinsmen who brought greetings from, and news of, friends and relatives. We were always glad to see them. They would stay for days, according to the Kiowa notion of a proper visit.

It was not until later that I became aware of the real significance of these reunions and visitations. They were matters of ancient tradition and necessity. In the heyday of the plains culture, the tribe was composed of bands, each one going its own way. The essential integrity of the tribe was maintained by means of a kind of institutionalized visiting, whereby persons and families would venture abroad to pay visits, to keep intact a whole network of news and trade. This communion was of course a principal function of the annual Sun Dance as well.

The visitors I liked best, besides the children of my own age, were the old people, for they were exotic. They wore their hair in braids, both men and women, they spoke only Kiowa, and they imaged for me the bygone and infinitely exciting time of the centaurs, the warriors, and the buffalo hunters.

Among the visitors in my father's day was the old man Koi-khan-hodle, "Dragonfly," who to pay his respects every morning would get up before dawn, paint his face, and go out to pray aloud to the rising sun. I have stood on the red earth just east of the house where Koi-khan-hodle stood; I have seen across the plain to the edge of the world; and there I have seen the sun rise. And it was for me the deity that it was for Dragonfly. In that image is concentrated for me the great mystery of the Sun Dance, the long migration of the Kiowas to their destiny, and the tenure of my people on this continent, a tenure of many thousands of years.

When I was a child there was a red barn a little to the north and east of the house, near the place where Koi-khan-hodle made his prayer. I loved to play in the barn, which seemed a great cavern of possibility. There, in the dim light, lay a box of bones, the bones of a horse. The horse, called "Gudal-san" never lost a race. That its bones should be kept long after its death seems entirely appropriate in the context of the plains culture. The Kiowas owned more horses *per capita* than any other tribe on the Great Plains. There is no story of the Kiowa without the horse.

Off the southwest corner of the house, near the kitchen steps, was the storm cellar. On the surface it was an earthen mound supported by concrete or cement, I believe, with a large wooden trapdoor at the end nearer the house, slanted at perhaps twenty or thirty degrees. Beneath this door concrete steps led down into a small, subterranean room outfitted with a bench, and little if anything else. In the springtime, when storms raged on the plains, my mother would take me and a kerosene lamp down into that gravelike room in which the earth had a smell that I have never known elsewhere. With the wind roaring and rain—sometimes earsplitting hail—pounding at the door, my mother would read to soothe her frayed nerves, and I would fall asleep in spite of the fury. My father, who had a Kiowa indifference to such weather, could not be bothered to join us.

The arbor was the center of summer. When the weather turned hot we lived in the arbor. It was a sizable frame building, open and screened on all sides, so that the air could move through it freely. It was basically one great room, though a small kitchen extended from the northwest corner. When it rained, water came in from the roof and all around. There was a large table in the middle of the red earthen floor, large enough to seat a dozen people easily. Along the south and east walls were broad wooden benches. On these we slept at night. Along the north wall were cabinets in which were kept dishes and flatware, an ice box (I loved to go with my father to Mountain View, where we bought great blocks of ice), and a shelf on which were a bucket of water and a dipper for drinking and two or three metal basins for washing. When I was old and strong enough, I drew water from the well and carried it to its place on the shelf. There was no plumbing in those days, and no electricity. We walked to the outhouse, and we lighted the nights with kerosene lamps.

Most of the Kiowas in the vicinity, including my grandmother, were members of the Rainy Mountain Baptist Church congregation. There were prayer meetings in the arbor on summer nights, and these were wonderful occasions. The older people came in their finery, and they brought good food in abundance. They sang hymns in Kiowa, they gave testimony to their faith in the rich oratory of the Native American oral tradition—and they visited. The children played outside in the lamplight that fell upon the grass, caught up in the sheer excitement of communion, celebration, festivity. I can still hear the singing and the laughter and the lively talk floating on the plain, reaching away to the dark river and the pecan grove, reaching perhaps to Rainy Mountain and the old school and cemetery.

Home. Homestead. Ancestral home. If I close my eyes, I can see Dragonfly there beyond the hedge. I can see my young parents walking toward the creek in the late afternoon, a coppery light on the path. I can hear my grandmother's voice in the rooms of the house and in the cool corners of the arbor. And these are sacred recollections of the mind and heart.

part three

THE STORYTELLER
AND HIS ART

Introduction

There is only one story, after all, and it is about the pursuit of man by God, and it is about a man who ventures out to the edge of the world, and it is about his wife, who is faithful or unfaithful, and it is about the hunting of a great beast.

—The Ancient Child

To tell a story in the proper way, to hear a story told in the proper way—this is a very old and sacred business, and it is very good. At that moment when we are drawn into the element of language, we are as intensely alive as we can be; we create and we are created. That existence in the maze of words is our human condition. Because of language we are, among all the creatures in our world, the most dominant and the most isolated. Our dominance is supreme, and our isolation is profound. That equation is the very marrow of story. It is a story in itself. We have no being beyond our stories. Our stories explain us, justify us, sustain us, humble us, and forgive us. And sometimes they injure and destroy us. Make no mistake, we are at risk in the presence of words. Perhaps the greatest stories are those which disturb us, which shake us from our complacency, which threaten our well-being. It is better to enter into the danger of such a story than to keep safely away in a space where the imagination lies dormant.

But there are stories and there are stories. Our spirits are appropriately buoyed by story. Children delight in stories which excite the imagination, whether they disturb the peace of mind or not. Stories are sometimes informed with great delicacy and wonder. We are shaken and soothed in turn by stories. One of the principal rules of storytelling is that a balance must be struck. Perhaps the central function of storytelling is to reflect the forces, within and without us, that govern our lives, both good and bad. This is a very simple notion, but it is profound. Stories are pools of reflection in which we see ourselves through the prism of the imagination.

When the Stars Fell

When I was six months old I was given my Indian name, Tsoai-talee, by an old Kiowa man whose name was Pohd-lohk. He was an interesting man, and I have thought about him a good deal. Among the things that preoccupied Pohd-lohk was a notion of history. He began to deal with time, his old age, a restlessness. He kept a journal in which he recorded, in pictographs, events which marked the progress of his people from one point in time to another.

I have seen this calendar, and I have imagined Pohd-lohk at the task of keeping it; it must have been a sacred business.

He would go into the bedroom and close the door. From a bureau drawer he would remove a book and spectacles; these he kept always together. The book, a ledgerbook which he had obtained from the supply office at Fort Sill, was wrapped round with a red kerchief. It had been in his possession many years, and it meant something to him. He laid his hands on it in a certain way, with precise, familiar care. It was a calendar history of the Kiowa people from 1833. Pohd-lohk could not remember how it was that he came to his regard for history, nor why he determined to set it down in pictures on a page, but the book had become a serious affair in his life. At first he recorded events which had been preserved upon an older calendar, a hide painting, then the recollection of things that fell within the purview of his own memory. Now that he was old, he liked to look backward in time, and although he could neither read nor write, the calendar was his means. It was an instrument with which he could reckon his place in the world, as if he could see there the long swath of his coming and going and feel in his veins a force that had been set in motion before he was born. Anterior to that, there was only mystery, a kind of prehistoric and impenetrable genesis, a reality of no particular shape, duration, or meaning beyond myth. He knew or cared very little about it: the Kiowas had entered the world; they had known suffering and triumph; and they had journeyed a long way from their place of origin. But it was all one moment to Pohd-lohk, as if everything, the whole world, had been created on that morning of November 13, 1833, when the sky was filled with a strange commotion of the stars—the most spectacular shower of Leonid meteors ever recorded.

He opened the book to the first page, and it was *De-pegya-de Sai*, November, 1833, and the stars were falling. He closed his eyes, the better to see them. They were everywhere in the darkness, so numerous and bright indeed that the night was shattered. They flew like sparks, he thought, and he thought also of slender, pointed leaves turning in the sun, and of pure light glittering upon water. But as he watched, dreaming, the stars were at last like nothing he had ever seen or would ever see beyond this, his imagination and the memory in his blood. Truly they were not like sparks or leaves or facets of light upon water. In some older and more nearly perfect synthesis of motion and light, the stars wheeled across the vision of his mind's eye. They pitched and veered; they drew near and loomed; and they fell slowly and silently away in the void. Silently. Men, women, and children were running here and there in the flashing light, their eyes wide and their mouths twisted with fear, but he could not hear their running, nor even the sound of their cries. And yet it did not seem strange to him that there should be no sound upon the scene. It was as if the earth—or even so much of it as he knew—had fallen off into the still, black depths. Even as this bright havoc was somehow the element of his perception just now, on the very edge of hallucination, so was silence the element in which the stars moved inexorably. They fell in long arcs and traces, bright delineations of time and space, describing eternity. He looked after them, to the edge of time and beyond.

Pohd-lohk died in 1939, before I could really know him. I think of him just so, taking leave of himself in his dreams, the old one who gave me my name.

The Indian Dog

When I was growing up I lived in a pueblo in New Mexico. There one day I bought a dog. I was twelve years old, the bright autumn air was cold and delicious, and the dog was an unconscionable bargain at five dollars.

It was an Indian dog; that is, it belonged to a Navajo man who had come to celebrate the Feast of San Diego. It was one of two or three rangy animals following in the tracks of the man's covered wagon as he took leave of our village on his way home. Indian dogs are marvelously independent and resourceful, and they have an idea of themselves, I believe, as knights and philosophers.

The dog was not large, but neither was it small. It was one of those unremarkable creatures that one sees in every corner of the world, the common denominator of all its kind. But on that day—and to me—it was noble and brave and handsome.

It was full of resistance, and yet it was ready to return my deep, abiding love; I could see that. It needed only to make a certain adjustment in its lifestyle, to shift the focus of its vitality from one frame of reference to another. But I had to drag my dog from its previous owner by means of a rope. It was nearly strangled in the process, its bushy tail wagging happily all the while.

That night I secured my dog in the garage, where there was a warm clean pallet, wholesome food, and fresh water, and I bolted the door. And the next morning the dog was gone, as in my heart I knew it would be; I had read such a future in its eyes. It had squeezed through a vent, an opening much too small for it, or so I had thought. But as they say, where there is a will there is a way—and the Indian dog was possessed of one indomitable will.

I was crushed at the time, but strangely reconciled, too, as if I had perceived intuitively some absolute truth beyond all the billboards of illusion.

The Indian dog had done what it had to do, had behaved exactly as it must, had been true to itself and to the sun and moon. It knew its place in the scheme of things, and its place was precisely there, with its right destiny, in the tracks of the wagon. In my mind's eye I could see it at that very moment, miles away, plodding in the familiar shadows, panting easily with relief, after a bad night, contemplating the wonderful ways of man.

Caveat emptor. But from that experience I learned something about the heart's longing. It was a lesson worth many times five dollars.

The Photograph

When I first lived on the Navajo reservation there were no cars, except those that were government property or that belonged to the Indian Service employees. The Navajos went about in wagons and on horseback, everywhere. My father worked for the Roads Department on the Navajo reservation. I lived for those trips, for he would often take me with him. I got a sense of the country then; it was wild and unending. In rainy weather the roads became channels of running water, and sometimes a flash flood would simply wash them away altogether, and we would have to dig ourselves out of the mud or wait for the ground to freeze. And then the wagons would pass us by or, if we were lucky, some old man would unhitch his team and pull us out to firm ground.

"*Ya'at'eeh,*" the old man would say.

"*Ya'at'eeh, shicheii,*" my father would reply.

"*Hagosha' diniya?*"

"Nowhere," my father would say, "we are going nowhere."

"*Aoo', atiin ayoo hastlish.*" Yes, the road is very muddy, the old man would answer, laughing, and we knew then that we were at his mercy, held fast in the groove of his humor and goodwill. My father learned to speak the Navajo language in connection with his work, and I learned something of it, too—a little. Later, after I had been away from the Navajo country for many years, I returned and studied the language formally in order to understand not only the meaning but the formation of it as well. It is a beautiful language, intricate and full of subtlety, and very difficult to learn.

There were sheep camps in the remote canyons and mountains. When we ventured out into those areas, we saw a lot of people, but they were always off by themselves, it seemed, living a life of their own, each one having an individual existence in that huge landscape. Later, when I was learning to fly an airplane, I saw the land as a hawk or an eagle sees it, immense and wild and all of a piece. Once I flew with a friend to the trading post at Low Mountain where we landed on a dirt road in the very middle of the reservation. It was like going backward in time, for Low Mountain has remained virtually undiscovered in the course of years, and there you can still see the old people coming in their wagons to get water and to trade. It is like Kayenta was in my earliest time on the reservation, so remote as to be almost legendary in the mind.

My father had a little box camera with which he liked to take photographs now and then. One day an old Navajo crone came to our house and asked to have her picture taken. She was a gnarled old woman with gray hair and fine pronounced features. She made a wonderful subject, and I have always thought very well of the photograph that my father made of her. Every day thereafter she would come to the house and ask to see the print, and every day my father had to tell her that it had not yet come back in the mail. Having photographs processed was a slow business then in that part of the world. At last the day came when the print arrived. And when the old woman came, my father presented it to her proudly. But when she took a look at it, she was deeply disturbed, and she would have nothing to do with it. She set up such a jabber, indeed, that no one could understand her, and she left in a great huff. I have often wondered that she objected so to her likeness, for it was a true likeness, as far as I could tell. It is quite possible, I think, that she had never seen her likeness before, not even in a mirror, and that the photograph was a far cry from what she imagined herself to be. Or perhaps she saw, in a way that we could not, that the photograph misrepresented her in some crucial respect, that in its dim, mechanical eye it had failed to see into her real being.

An Encounter in Greenland

One day last summer I traveled by boat along the far northwest coast of Greenland—to the little settlement of Siorpaluk, an Eskimo village about halfway between the Arctic Circle and the North Pole. It was bitterly cold on the water, and yet I could not bring myself to leave the deck, not even for the steaming hot tea below. For the world of that Arctic summer morning was ineffably beautiful. The sun set a glitter on the whole sea. The air was so crisp and clean that it seemed indivisible with the light; it seemed a cold emanation of the sun. The steep land lay off the starboard rail—blue and purple bluffs, and glaciers spilling down. And the whole way we steered barely clear of icebergs. They were huge, fantastic shapes, the size of great ships, the size of skyscrapers, full of iridescences.

At Siorpaluk I walked along a golden, crescent beach until I was just beyond the village. Some of the "calves" of the icebergs had been washed up there. They stood on the sand, creaking, cracking, sweating under the great weight of the sun. I paused at one, within arm's reach. It was the shape of a rabbit's head—about twice my size—its great ears askew and precariously pitched. It creaked and groaned. It would break apart any moment for sure. But nothing happened. Nothing happened, except that the thing crackled on. At last I decided to take matters into my own hands. I backed off, took up some stones from the beach, and hurled them at the thing. I couldn't miss, I was so close. But nothing happened. After ten minutes of this assault nothing happened. The thing stood shining and impervious before me.

Then I heard someone shouting behind me. Startled, I turned to see an old Eskimo hunter hurrying toward me, gesticulating wildly—carrying a rifle in his hands. I was terrified. He came upon me, talking now, excitedly, in his native tongue.

At last I understood. Did I want him to shoot the iceberg? I was greatly relieved, to be sure. I was humbled. I said yes, please. And he shot the iceberg. In the explosion a part of it went spinning off into the fjord. But still it was the shape of a rabbit's head.

The old man regarded me kindly for a moment, turned, and walked away to his shack. It seemed to me that his attitude was that of having done a good deed.

This is what he said to himself, I believe: "Look at this stranger, this man from some world beyond my ken, beyond my imagination; he comes here to my village, and immediately he tries to kill the icebergs. It seems a strange and futile enterprise. But he is a human being, as I am too. And I shall help him if I can."

A Turning Point

There was a time when my friend Nelson set himself upon a course of pure adventure. He wandered about the world in hot pursuit of himself. He fought bulls in Mexico, hunted for treasure in the South Seas, and punched cattle in the Outback. He was caught up in a maelstrom, or so it seemed to me. And yet I was green with envy.

His life seemed a series of high moments, moments of such intensity that his whole destiny might have been concentrated in each one of them. In those days I was struggling through school. The life of the mind seemed pale by comparison; I received Nelson's letters from the most exotic ports of call, and I suffered considerably.

Now and then our paths crossed. Nelson and I managed to have brief reunions in San Francisco, Charlottesville, New Orleans, Santa Fe. Always he had great stories to tell. I remember this one in particular:

"Well, my friend," he said to me one day. "I was walking along a dusty road in northern Spain when a Gypsy cart, drawn by a mule, passed me by. I paid not much attention to it at first, you understand, but when I looked up I saw that the driver was a young man of no particular distinction—and that his wife, who was sitting at his back on a bed of straw, was the most beautiful woman I had ever seen. She was looking straight at me and smiling. Oh, my friend, how I loved her!—completely, do you see? And a more perfect love there never was. I thought, I should certainly challenge this man, do him in, and run away with his wife. But I did nothing of the sort. I walked on, looking after my true love and losing ground, until the cart was out of sight."

Well, that was Nelson's story. When I heard it I was greatly surprised by the ending. My imagination had already proceeded to the challenge, the duel in the sun, and the flight of the lovers into the mountains. But the story I heard is a better one than the one I had in mind. There is more truth to it, at last, more of human nature. I have told it to others, and their reaction is always the same: they have the sense that it is their story, that their daily lives are made up of such stories—or of this very one, perhaps, told over and over again.

Anyway, Nelson called me on the telephone last evening, rather late. He had drunk a rare and delicious wine, and he came through in a high, euphoric mood. As always, we spoke of many things. And then I reminded him of this "episode of the highway," this Spanish tragedy.

"I remember, of course," he said.

"It is a memorable story," I agreed. "And it seems moreover to have been a crucial moment in your life, a turning point."

"Yes, that's right..."

I knew that I was pressing, but I couldn't help myself. "I wonder what might have become of you, had you stolen the woman and run away with her," I mused.

"Yes, I wonder," he said. His voice seemed suddenly far away.

"Hmm. Why didn't you, do you suppose?"

"Because I was twenty-five," he replied, "and full of understanding." Then wistfully, "If only I had been twenty and known nothing."

There was an appropriate silence between us, full of understanding, and then we went on to other things.

Quincy Tahoma

I came to know Quincy Tahoma long after I had lived on the Navajo reservation, but he brought that landscape back to me in all his ways. He was essentially a Navajo of the old order, and he reminded me of the very old men I had seen at Shiprock and Tuba City and Chinle when I was a child. There was a mighty reserve in him, and a quiet dignity that was impressive in itself. He died as a young man of alcoholism, so they say. I wonder if he did not actually die of a broken heart. It seemed to me that he had been severed for many years in his mind from the world in which his roots were planted. This is not a rare affliction among Indians, especially those who have the old ways fixed forever in their blood.

Quincy was born in Arizona on the Navajo reservation at Cornfields. Once he told me this: that he was extremely ill as an infant and that no one supposed that he would live through the first winter of his life. Consequently his parents wrapped him in a blanket and placed him in the snow to die. But he did not die, and at last a relative—an aunt, as I remember—picked him up out of the snow and carried him home with her. He grew up under the stigma of having been abandoned, "thrown away," as the Kiowas would say, and he was made to keep away from the center of family life and to play an inferior part in family affairs. A great, dark loneliness seemed pervasive in him, deep down at the very center of his being, too intrinsic to be relieved. You could see this in him, at moments, when he fell silent; there was then a quality of distance upon him, as if he were gone far away from you in his thoughts.

In his stature, too, there was something of the outcast. He was of medium height, and somewhat thickset, but in his movements there was a kind of slow and angular aspect, like the shadow of an old impairment in his limbs—in his arms, especially, which seemed less developed than his body. His hands were small and delicate, and he held them always gracefully; he thought very well of his hands.

Quincy knew nothing of the wider world until he went away to school as a young man. He attended the Santa Fe Indian School, which is now the Institute of American Indian Arts, and there he gave himself up to painting and became a fine artist. His paintings are highly prized now, and indeed they should be, for they are remarkable evocations of the Navajo world.

He told a good story on himself. When he first went to the Santa Fe Indian School, everything was new to him, and he had no notion of how to behave, and so he got on by imitating his fellows. On Sunday mornings the students were encouraged to attend religious services in the auditorium. On the occasion of his first attendance, there was offered up a Catholic mass, and he went through the motions as best he could, sitting, standing, and kneeling after the example of the congregation. But when it came time for communion, there occurred for Quincy a kind of crisis: half the people proceeded to the communion rail, and half did not. He elected to join the communicants.

"At first I did not know what to do," he said. "But then it became clear to me that food was being offered to us, and that it would be an impolite thing to refuse. And anyway, I was hungry."

When I lived with my parents at Jemez Pueblo, Quincy came there a number of times to visit. My father had a small studio at one corner of the house, and when Quincy came the two of them secluded themselves there and painted, side by side, instructing each other in what they knew. They got on very well, and their meetings must have been valuable as well as congenial to them both. There were long silences, then low, indistinct talk in that room, and every so often a great eruption of laughter, which was always a great frustration to me. As with Indians in general, Quincy had a fine sense of humor and a good way with words.

At the end of the day the two men would emerge from the studio in a high, euphoric mood, ready for anything. Most often they would go off into the Jemez Mountains and cook meat on an open fire, and more often than not they would take me with them. Those were great occasions for me, for I was let into the inner circle, as it were. Night fell as the meat was cooking, and the mountain air was always fresh and cold, and it made a mighty hunger in me. Quincy and my father talked on in the manner of old Indian men, slowly, easily, with an indigenous, high order of wit and wisdom. I settled into their language, and I was at ease there.

Jay Silverheels

Harold J. Smith died the other day. I suspect that few, if any, people knew him by that name. He was better known as Jay Silverheels, American Indian actor, who appeared in such popular films as *Broken Arrow, Walk the Proud Land, True Grit,* and *The Man Who Loved Cat Dancing.* But without doubt he was best known as Tonto, faithful companion to the Lone Ranger, masked rider of the plains, who for a generation or two (including mine) was seen in the mind's eye to race upon the great horse Silver—to the lyrical intensity of the *William Tell* Overture—directly into the moral fray, again and again. And again and again Tonto saved the day. He said things like "me not kill," and "here come chief, Kimosabe," and "Gettum-up, Scout!" If I remember rightly he was most often a double agent, trading upon his keen insight into the two worlds in confrontation in the Wild West. Always, of course, he lived in the shadow of the Lone Ranger, but he didn't mind. Ambition and competition, in the white man's terms, were of no use to him. One supposes that his lifestyle was very clean and simple, remarkably free of moral or psychological or even clerical—especially clerical—ambiguities. For those of us who first encountered Tonto on the radio, it could not be seriously doubted that he ate Wheaties for breakfast, or that he was kind to his horse and to widows and orphans.

Jay Silverheels became Tonto in 1949. He appeared in all 221 episodes of ABC's *Lone Ranger* series on television. To the old audible dimension of Tonto's broken English there was added the visual aspect of the dark, straight, athletic man in headband and fringed buckskins. We recognized him at once.

There was a real man behind the popular image, and a good one. Jay

Silverheels was a Mohawk Indian, born in 1920 on the Six Nations Reservation in Ontario. Physically he was quick and lithe and powerful. He raced horses in harness, he boxed in Golden Gloves tournaments, and he came to Hollywood in 1933 as the member of a touring professional lacrosse team.

In terms of talent, he gave precisely what he was asked to give. He might have given more, had Hollywood's notion of cowboys and Indians been more creative, imaginative, and responsible. He worked tirelessly to help other Indians become actors. In the late sixties he founded the Indian Actors Workshop in Hollywood, and he insisted that the studios for which he worked hire Indians to play Indian parts.

Jay Silverheels suffered a stroke in 1980 and died shortly thereafter of pneumonia and complications.

As for me, I shall remember him as Tonto, that figment of the American imagination. For it is not a bad thing, after all, to have some stake in legend, and Tonto and his friend—what's his name?—are surely the stuff of legend. And they will certainly outlive us all, and that is as it should be.

I once read a piece by Franz Kafka in which he suggested that Don Quixote was the lesser part of Sancho Panza—something to that effect—and that Sancho Panza followed Don Quixote on his mad exploits out of a sense of responsibility, delighting in his charge, as a parent might follow a child on its explorations through the park. If Tonto is a figment of the American imagination, I wonder, isn't it possible that the Lone Ranger is a figment of Tonto's imagination?

One Morning in Oklahoma

One summer I was walking in Oklahoma, at the foot of the Wichita Mountains. The place had been made into a park, a game preserve. It was July, and the grasses were high, bristling, and sunburnt, crackling with grasshoppers and bees. At midmorning the light was intense, and the air was sultry and full of radiance. The sky was as deep as I had ever seen it. There were wildflowers all around, brilliant points and pools of color. The sense of summer was pervasive and absolute.

The calf lay in a hollow of the meadow, its mother standing a few feet away and grazing, her great, shaggy head bent to the ground. She seemed utterly careless and content, and she paid me no mind, as far as I could tell. The calf was very beautiful, soft and supple with new life, perfectly composed in sleep. It was nearly orange in color, with white at its underside and black at its ears, nose, and hooves. I marveled at it and drew closer.

Suddenly the cow was there, looming huge above her calf, poised and tense, her head slung low, regarding me sideways. Her nostrils flared, and I could see the whites of her eyes. I wheeled, even as she lunged, and ran as hard as I could. She did not pursue me more than a few steps. The whole thing was a gesture on her part, but a very grand and decisive one, and I understood it well enough. I had crossed the boundary of her sacred domain, had entered into her sphere of instinct and taken leave of my own. This sort of thing one does at his peril.

I Wonder What Will Happen to the Land

I wonder what will happen to the land. There are others, too, who wonder. I see them walking here and there, in the early morning or evening, among the hills. They walk slowly, and they seem lost in thought. Now and then they pause in their going and bend down to look at wildflowers or into pools that stand in the arroyos after rain.

When I lived at Jemez, I used to walk along a dirt road that led away to the river. At evening there were wagons on the road, and men and boys coming home from the fields. I would greet them, and go upon my way. In summer and autumn, especially, the land had a great liveliness to it. Birds hurtled in the sky and rabbits ran in the brush. On either side of the road you could see squash and melons among the leaves that were low to the ground; and bunches of grapes, too, upon the vines, and ears of colored corn upon the stalks. In late summer the corn grew to eye level, and you could look across a plane of tassels shimmering in the air, as water shimmers.

Most often I would stop at the river and stand for a time on the water's edge, on a bank that was cobbled with smooth stones, and watch out for the coming of dusk. Beyond the river, westward, was a peneplain of many colors, and at evening the colors changed before your eyes. The plain reached away until, in the distance, it was broken into dunes, lavender and blue and gray, dotted with dark growth, and then the farther mesas and the mountains, standing against the sky. Evening was like a thin smoke upon the mountains; in it they loomed in darkness and in depth, like the mouth of a great cave, and the skyline grew soft, as if it had been a line drawing in charcoal. By degrees, the middle distance receded into a single shadow, like the endless rain shadow of a continent.

It has been some time, now, since I walked upon that road, but I remember it very well, and I take delight in remembering.

Landscapes tend to stand out in my memory. When I think back to a particular time in my life, I tend to see it in terms of its setting, the background in which it achieves for me a certain relief. Or to put it another way, I am inclined closely to associate events with the physical dimensions in which they take place. Perhaps this is true of most of us, but I have become in recent years more and more conscious of this associative process and of its implications.

Events take place. How many times have I used this expression, and how often have I stopped to think what it means? Events do indeed take place; they bear meaning in relation to the things around them. And I, too, happen to take place, each day of my life, in my environment. I exist in a landscape, and my existence is indivisible with the land.

But I wonder what will happen to the land—and, consequently, to my existence within it. It is changing from day to day, and faster than I like to think. This change, visible as it is and irrevocable as it seems to be, is one of the more ominous signs of the times. Today there is a school, a supermarket, a filling station where yesterday there was a wood or an open field.

Land development is a prevalent concept these days, and we have derived it honestly enough. It is a concept that is very much in keeping with the general ethic of our society. We are expansive and utilitarian as a people; our business is to make progress, to harvest our natural resources, and to develop change. And we are apparently good at it. But it occurs to me that development is too often a euphemism for the manufacture of waste. Profit is high and conservation low on our list of priorities. What we have developed all too frequently is not the land, but a crisis in our relationship to the land, a state of emergency.

I have a recurrent dream—a kind of nightmare—in which I am engaged in conversation with one Mr. Greed, the president of a development company. The conversation is purely academic, for Mr. Greed's plans to build a multilevel parking lot on Apodaca Hill have already been approved, and indeed construction has begun. We have to speak above the noise of earth-moving machines.

"Why here?" I ask. "Why did you choose this location, Mr. Greed?"

He looks at me as if I am mad, and he replies, "Because I was attracted by the beauty of the land."

The Toll Road

I know a man who runs every morning. He runs into the foothills, where there are deep, many-colored folds in the earth and there are many more rabbits than people. The running, it may be, satisfies some longing in his breast.

He told me this story, which I relate in his own words.

"For some time, several weeks, I ran on the road that lies in the hills to the south. I like to run early in the morning, as you know, when the skyline is a silhouette and there are long shadows in my way—shadows within shadows—like deep, dark pools of water. It is a wonderful time to regard the earth, and a wonderful way to be in touch with it; I tell you, it is a religious experience I'm talking about, a holy thing.

"Well, one morning, after I had been following the same course for many days and had established a clear right-of-way, so to speak, I was amazed to find that someone had placed a barrier across the road, a bundle of branches! Oh, it was nothing that I couldn't negotiate with ease, mind you—it was only a token, after all. But the point is, it was there. It threatened me in some way, stood against me, destroyed the rhythm of my running...and of my life. I had to deal with it, don't you see? I removed it."

He paused here. I had become keenly interested in the story. It had begun to take the shape of a riddle, I thought. I asked him to go on.

"At first I supposed that the barrier was a joke or an accident," he said. "I thought that perhaps it had fallen from a wagon. I didn't want to take it personally, you see. But it was there again the next morning, and again I removed it. Every day it was there, and every day I removed it. Then I had to admit that the barrier was *mine*, that it was placed there every day for no other purpose than to deter, impede, irritate, and finally infuriate *me*.

"Well, at last I discovered who my antagonist was, an elderly Indian man who lived nearby. His father probably lived there before him, and his father's father. He had no deed to the land, you know, but it was his all the same, by right of possession. He had centered his whole life upon it. In his eyes I was merely some pest, some vagrant—but eminently more dangerous than most because I had set up a continuum of intrusion, a persistent encroachment upon his domain, spiritual as well as physical. I never saw him, and as far as I know he never saw me, but we were engaged in a skirmish of the soul.

"On Christmas morning I took a bottle of wine with me into the hills. I removed the barrier which, sure enough, my adversary had again laid in my way, and I left the bottle of wine in its place.

"Not since has there been a barrier there, and every morning now I have only the open road before me and the sunlight breaking upon the red earth. I am free to run on the road, having paid my way, don't you see? And I have no complaints. It was a reasonable fee, after all—oh, a token—to be sure but, you know, there are times when nothing is so valuable as a token. I am convinced that a handkerchief or a robin's egg or a sack of tobacco would have sufficed as well. The important thing is that I acknowledged the old man's possession of the land. That's all he wanted."

Graceful and At Ease

When she was a young woman, Karen Blixen, later known as Isak Dinesen, went to live on a coffee plantation in Africa. Years later, when she had returned to her native Denmark, she wrote of her life on the farm in Kenya and of the East African landscape. *Out of Africa*, published in 1937, is one of the great books of our time, I believe. I would not presume to say why it is great; there are probably many reasons, and no doubt they have all more or less to do with that ineffable quality which we call genius. But one of the reasons is surely this: that Karen Blixen entered so completely into the landscape of the place that it became at last the landscape of the spirit. This is not an easy transformation to make, and it is not easy to understand. It is as if the very soil itself had never really existed, until it came to exist in the writer's particular expression of it.

She wrote short stories as well, marvelously intricate fantasies that are as rare, faceted, and gleaming as gems. They take hold of the imagination. They seem to verify that literature is, after all, nothing so much as profound consolation. "All sorrows can be borne," she said, "if you put them into a story, or tell a story about them." This was a principle of her life.

She visited the United States in the late 1950s, shortly before her death. It pleased her to gather people about her, and when she spoke to them she most often began by saying, "Let me tell you a story." I never met her, but I have often wished that I had been in her audience on one of those occasions. It would have been a large moment in my life, I am sure.

Her own story was a tragic one, in many respects. It involved her father's suicide, a brief and unhappy marriage, the loss of a lover, a fatal disease, and a long dying. But above all it involved her life in Africa.

There are some remarkable photographs of Karen Blixen. In one, she is standing in her riding habit, holding a huge rose, on the African farm in 1919. Beside her is the silhouette of Dusk, her Scotch deerhound. She stands graceful and at ease in a frame of dense foliage. She is uncommonly beautiful.

In another, a profile taken by Cecil Beaton in New York forty years later, she is the very image of a witch, something out of *Macbeth* or the mythologies of voodoo. There is a certain mirth at her mouth—and she has the devil in her eyes. Surely some fantastic tale is running through her head.

The great house at Ngong has come to be called Karen House, and Karen Estate is now a suburb of Nairobi. When she left Africa, as she did once and for all in 1931, she took with her a small box of African earth. It was mixed with the soil of Zealand in her grave in Denmark.

An Element of Piety

Cacique del Monte Chamiza is a twenty-month-old black Labrador retriever. He lives in my house and is the darling of my daughters. His name, unwieldy if not downright pretentious, is a kind of concession to his breeding. His dam is a champion of the arena, and his sire is famous for his work in the field. But Cacique does not bargain on the strength of his pedigree; nor does he seem to place much stock in the conjugation of names and identities. He seems to know who he is, and he is comfortable in the world.

He is good-natured in the extreme. Indeed, goodness is so intrinsic to his nature that it would be hard to find room for other attributes in his character; he is essentially, definitively good. It may well be that Cacique del Monte Chamiza is good to a fault.

Of late he has assumed a certain posture with respect to others of his kind. He has, I believe, conceived a holier-than-thou notion of himself. An element of piety has entered into his being. And like learning, a little piety is a dangerous thing.

It all came about some time ago, on one January 17th, the feast of St. Anthony, Abbot, to be precise. At five o'clock in the afternoon on that day, Father Benedict Cuesta, pastor of Cristo Rey Church, administered a blessing to the animals of the parish, Cacique among them. It was a memorable occasion. Dusk was descending quickly upon the adobe walls and crept like smoke in the earthen streets; there was a fine edge on the air—and a fragrance of woodsmoke and of good food cooking on Apodaca Hill. The sunset was soft and full of silence, with no glisten or glare upon it, only a wide, irregular band of gunmetal on the Jemez range. It was not especially cold.

From all directions came the animals. At last they were assembled at the front door of the great church: cats and dogs, chickens and ducks, horses and goats. A diminutive, black-eyed girl held an enormous muff to her chin; it turned out to be a white rabbit with a bubblegum-colored nose. It was rumored among the onlookers that a small boy near the front, named Alfredo, carried a white rat named Nicolas in his pocket. An elderly couple with no pet of their own moved from creature to creature, exclaiming with wonder and delight:

"Perfecto, look! What a *fine*-looking goat!"

"Oh, just see the kittens, Maria!"

"Splendid! Splendid!"

My daughters arrived, holding on to a taut leash, engaged in a desperate tug of war with Cacique the Unruly and (as yet) Unblessed. He had taken stock of the situation at once, perceived especially that there were chickens and cats upon the scene, and he was ready to impose himself like a bolt of lightning into their midst. What an irony that he should come to church of all places, I thought, this rowdy black profligate, even now about to shatter the ecclesiastical peace with the sheer force of his inexhaustible good will.

Then Father Cuesta appeared, and a remarkable calm fell upon the churchyard and the throng within. He passed among the faithful, so to speak, touching them with holy water and uttering the formula that would, in a sense, stand forever between them and the perils of paganism. Even Cacique was suddenly and appropriately meek, though in all honesty it ought to be pointed out that his restraint might have been due in part to the presence of a mature Saint Bernard, which had stepped down from a Volkswagen and loomed menacingly close by, holding Cacique quite still and docile in its gaze.

That's all. It was not exactly a crucial moment in the history of Western civilization, but it seems to have brought about a modest change in the climate of my own household at least. Only yesterday, for example, an immense, brindled Great Dane came into our yard. To my utter amazement, Cacique lunged at the trespasser, snarling. The Great Dane was, I think, every bit as amazed as I and departed forthwith in order to ponder the madness in the world. Had I been Cacique, I would have been inclined to keep the peace, and I told him so. But then it occurred to me: perhaps Cacique has more spiritual change in his pocket than I have in mine. In any case, I am not the stuff of which martyrs are made.

Chopetl

The other evening, while perusing a set of Territorial documents, I read with keen interest the following notice, which appeared in *The New Mexican* of February 27, 1872:

> Half a dozen noisy and disorderly vagabonds were arrested last night by the police. One of them had a heavy slingshot secured to his wrist by a thong, and was evidently prepared for anything bad. They were all to be taken before a magistrate for examination this morning.

There is an unusual story here. The slingshot—actually, it is a dullimer—has been in my possession for many years. It was given to me by the late Colonel Otto Firpo on the occasion of my tenth birthday. Otto was the son of Viktor Maximilian Firpo, the explorer—and the man mentioned above. Far from being a vagabond, he was among the wealthiest and most accomplished men of his era. It is true, however, that he hated all notoriety with a passion, and, from an early age, strove to be anonymous in all his affairs. He became a master of disguise, so successful indeed that history has been confounded. No biographer has dared to attempt even so much as an outline of Firpo's life, so much does it consist in bits and pieces.

In January 1872, for example, Viktor Firpo led an archeological expedition into the Valley of Mexico. As usual, we have only skeletal information: the expedition was attacked by savages and decimated; Viktor wrested from one of his assailants the dullimer, a legendary weapon of the Stone Age, and, turning it against his adversaries, drove them away; one month later to the day, Viktor Firpo and five others, the sole survivors, entered into the holy city of Santa Fe at night; one of their number, apparently stricken with a rare fever, cried out in delirium and created a disturbance; the party was apprehended in the vicinity of Burro Alley and placed under arrest; soon thereafter they were released in good health and high spirits.

The record shows that the leader of this strange retinue was one Carlos de los Angeles, twenty-three, a student at the University of Guadalajara. In point of fact, Firpo was in his seventy-ninth year at the time, and he had been twice around the world.

The dullimer is now one of two known to exist, the second having been unearthed in the excavations at Coatepec in 1958; it is preserved in the vault of the Bank of Veracruz at Jalapa Enríquez. Mine is, I believe, the better example of the armorer's art, especially with respect to the amulet, a leather bracelet to which the dullimer can be affixed and by means of which it can be activated with remarkable dispatch and efficiency, even while the bearer's hands are otherwise engaged. It is a truly formidable weapon, used, according to oral tradition, to fell even the great beasts of the jungle. I myself became somewhat proficient in its use for a time, and when called upon to demonstrate its effectiveness, I was pleased to do so. But one day I laid the dullimer to rest once and for all. I had a dream in which it seemed to me that I could decipher the ancient markings on the amulet:

> I, Chopetl, am grown weary of war;
> I have been deadly even to the gods.

Teresita

Edmund Wilson (1895–1972) was one of the foremost literary figures of his time. So great is his continuing influence upon modern letters that it seems strange now to refer to him in the past tense. For two generations at least, my own included, he seemed a kind of permanent— and formidable—presence upon the literary scene, a man whose critical intelligence had been brought to bear on the whole spectrum of literature. His judgment, whether you agreed with him or not, had to be reckoned with.

Although he was a poet, a playwright, and a novelist, Wilson made his most durable mark as a critic. In *Axel's Castle* (1931), he dealt incisively with the French Symbolists and their influence upon Yeats, Eliot, and Joyce, among others. In *The Wound and the Bow* (1941), he returned to Joyce and rendered both an explication and critique of *Finnegans Wake*. In *Patriotic Gore* (1962), he focused his attention sharply upon the literature of the American Civil War. These are clear and monumental works.

As a graduate student I became interested in the poems of Frederick Goddard Tuckerman, a New Englander of the nineteenth century whose work is informed by an extraordinary perception of the physical world. Tuckerman was a student of astronomy and botany as well as of literature, and his view of nature was based upon the principle of scientific observation. He could describe a natural setting, or some minute detail within it, with remarkable accuracy and precision.

My interest in Tuckerman was due in part to Edmund Wilson. He had discussed some of Tuckerman's poems in *Patriotic Gore*, and he had recognized Tuckerman's particular genius. When I finished my edition of Tuckerman's complete poems, I sent the manuscript to Wilson, who took it upon himself to place it with a publisher.

During the 1960s, Wilson and I carried on a correspondence. In a letter dated June 6, 1963, he wrote, "I used to know the Jemez Pueblo—back in about 1930. There was a beautiful Indian girl there named Teresita, the daughter of a well-known Indian politician. If you should meet her, please remember me to her." I received the letter at my parents' home at Jemez Springs. I knew most of the people of Jemez Pueblo, having lived there as a boy. I have not with certainty been able to identify Edmund Wilson's Teresita.

In his long lifetime Wilson knew a great many people and traveled widely over the earth. Moreover, his mind was surely populated with innumerable personages, fictitious as well as real, characters who inhabit the calligraphy of ancient scrolls and the milieu of modern film, in several languages, over twenty centuries. It fascinates me that he should recall to mind a girl in the Jemez Mountains across a span of thirty years. But why should it?

If in August, some year, when I go to see the Pecos bull run through the streets of Jemez Pueblo, I find the old woman Teresita, I shall indeed remember him to her.

The Head of a Man

The sky is blue, and the leaves of the trees are green. It might be summer; but on the other hand, if you look closely, the leaves are tinted with russet at the edges, and they droop on the limbs. The air curdles; here and there are little gusts of wind, spinning on the dusty lawns, scattering debris. It is winter, after all. A huge cat enters the yard: how softly it walks against the wind, all of its attitudes concentrated in stealth! Perhaps it is a philanderer, and its name is George or Geoffrey Talbot. Of course its name might be Evangeline Blaine; it is hard to say.

Mrs. Archuleta is a beautiful old woman. She comes to clean my house on Tuesdays. Always we speak in Spanish, with great, formal courtesy. Has she always been so much in possession of herself, so gracious and genteel? I try to imagine her as a child, but the child that comes to mind is very pensive and composed, sits very still upon a velvet cushion. I wonder why she doesn't run and play. "Would you like to play a game?" I ask. "Hide-and-seek, or ring-around-the rosy?" After a moment she replies sweetly, *"No, muchas gracias, señor; tengo algo que hacer."* She is beautiful and frail, and there is something like a pane of glass between us. And the next time I see Mrs. Archuleta I say, "Please forgive me; I have failed to imagine you correctly." But, unaccountably, I say it in English, and she does not comprehend my meaning. *"Sí, hace buen tiempo,"* she replies.

I read somewhere that "Man feeds wild horses to dogs and whales to cats." It is a sad, telling summation, like an epitaph. Once on a high hill at dusk I saw horses, five or six of them, running far below in a cavernous, smoky depression of the world. They seemed to describe the whole, hard energy of meteors, or that of a sharp, percussive music. And once, in the Santa Barbara Channel, I saw the hump of a gray whale emerge and submerge only yards away from me when I was riding in a small boat. It thrilled and frightened me at the same time, and afterward I felt a strange and unreasonable loneliness, as if some profound isolation had been confirmed forever there in the dark troughs of the sea.

I draw with charcoal the head of a man in profile. He gazes downward, toward something that I cannot see, something that lies apart from the picture plane. It is a manuscript, perhaps, or a chessboard, or the Battle of Maldon. There is nothing to indicate who, or what, or where the man is—and this pleases me, inasmuch as he himself seems pleased. There is a look of mild amusement at his mouth, as if in a moment he will surely smile. But there is no laughter in him. He has a high forehead and long, unkempt hair which gathers in black tangles and hanks about his dome. There is a heaviness to his face, a swelling upon his eyelids, a certain sag to his cheek and jowl; his lips are thick and sensuous, drawn back into a fold of flesh that hoods his chin. And yet his expression is hard, as if the foundation upon which his flesh rests cannot be shaken by what he sees. I like him immensely and feel that I have known him for many years, but only as an inscrutable reflection of my own uncertainty.

The Physicians of Trinidad

Rosa Maria Segale was born in Cicagna, Italy, in 1850. When she was four years old her family moved to America and settled in Cincinnati, Ohio. There, in 1866, Rosa entered the motherhouse of the Sisters of Charity and began a long and eventful religious life as Sister Blandina Segale, S. C. She was a member of this society for three quarters of a century; she died in Cincinnati in 1941, one month after her ninety-first birthday.

Sister Blandina was missioned to the West in 1872, and she lived for twenty-one years in the Territories of Colorado and New Mexico. During this period of time she kept a diary, which was published in 1932 under the title *At the End of the Santa Fe Trail*.

"Your real danger is from cowboys," she was told when she set out for the little town of Trinidad, Colorado, in the winter of 1872. "No virtuous woman is safe near a cowboy." And yet Sister Blandina seemed utterly fearless on the frontier.

She first met Billy the Kid at Trinidad in 1876, under strange circumstances. It is a good story, and an interesting variation on the old theme of the dying cowboy. Here are the particulars.

A man named Schneider, a member of the notorious gang led by Billy the Kid, appeared in Trinidad, mortally wounded. There he remained until he died, a period of several months. During this time Sister Blandina became Schneider's friend and confidante. To her he confessed a number of heinous crimes. One day he announced to her excitedly that Billy the Kid and other members of the gang were coming on Saturday afternoon at two o'clock. They were coming to scalp the four physicians of Trinidad, he said, for the reason that none of them had been good enough to treat his wound. Sister Blandina was horrified, and she allowed that she would most certainly be there on Saturday in order to confront the gang of outlaws in Schneider's room. His friends would be delighted to meet her, Schneider said; he had told them a good deal about her.

Saturday at the appointed time she entered the room to find the gang gathered about Schneider's bed. Introductions were made. Afterward Sister Blandina wrote in her diary, "The leader, Billy, has steel-blue eyes, peach complexion, is young, one would take him to be seventeen— innocent-looking, save for the corners of his eyes, which tell a set purpose, good or bad."

Billy the Kid was extremely courteous to her. "We are all glad to see you, Sister, and I want to say it would give me pleasure to be able to do you any favor."

"Yes, there is a favor you can grant me," replied the nun.

"The favor is granted," said the outlaw. And so the physicians of Trinidad, all four of them, were spared. Perhaps the considerable generosity of the moment was lost upon them, I don't know. But it was not lost upon Sister Blandina. She was moved to philosophical reflection: "Life is a mystery," she wrote in her diary. "What of the human heart? A compound of goodness and wickedness. Who has ever solved the secret of its workings? I thought: one moment diabolical, the next angelical."

Soon thereafter Sister Blandina was sent to continue her good work in Santa Fe, City of the Holy Faith. There, four years after their first encounter, she met Billy the Kid for the second and last time. The circumstances were different. Billy was a prisoner. On May 16, 1881, she wrote:

> I have just returned from the jail. The two prisoners were chained hands and feet, but the "Kid" besides being cuffed hands and feet, was also fastened to the floor. You can imagine the extreme discomfort of the position. When I got into the prison cell and "Billy" saw me, he said—as though we had met yesterday instead of four years ago—"I wish I could place a chair for you, Sister."

Though Billy the Kid was killed two months later, Sister Blandina must not have heard of his death until several weeks had passed, for it was September 8 when she wrote at Albuquerque, "Poor, poor 'Billy the Kid' was shot by Sheriff Patrick F. Garrett of Lincoln County."

Sister Blandina Segale, when she left New Mexico Territory, returned to live out her life in Ohio. In those later years she must have dreamed now and then of Billy the Kid. In her old age, when she was eighty-nine or ninety, I wonder if there were not times when she entered into a dimly lighted room, and there a boy—forever a boy, shackled to a moment remote but in her mind—smiled, spoke kindly to her, and placed a chair, gently, gently at her back.

The Dark Priest of Taos

As have others, I first encountered this dark, enigmatic man in the pages of Willa Cather's *Death Comes for the Archbishop*. I sense that Cather herself did not know quite what to make of him, this tyrannical and renegade priest, and so she is reportorial on the whole, fairly objective—but nearly evasive—in her treatment of him. But she is fascinated, too:

> At the moment of the Elevation the dark priest seemed to give his whole force, his swarthy body and all its blood, to that lifting-up. Rightly guided, the Bishop reflected, this Mexican might have been a great man. He had an altogether compelling personality, a disturbing, mysterious, magnetic power.

But for the bishop's reflection, which is incidental, here are dimensions of heroism. Padre Martinez resembles the Satan of *Paradise Lost*. But his story wants the structure of epic; he is a tragic figure in a play that is at last less than tragedy.

Antonio Jose Martinez was born at the end of the eighteenth century at Abiquiu, and there he grew up without benefit of reading and writing. He married at twenty and sired a daughter, but soon thereafter his wife and child died. He decided then to become a priest, and he entered a seminary in Mexico, where he was encouraged to develop the extraordinary powers of his mind. He became a brilliant scholar and was ordained after six years of study. In 1826 he received an appointment as pastor to the parish of Taos.

Of the next thirty years we have in the accessible volumes only the monumental facts of his life, and disparate details. In 1856 he tendered his resignation of the parish of Taos to Bishop Lamy on grounds of old age and infirmity. Thereafter, serious differences of opinion grew up between Padre Martinez and his successor, Father Demaso Taladrid. Though officially retired, Padre Martinez continued to say the mass, and he officiated over parish affairs when it pleased him to do so. At last there came about a rupture that was not to be tolerated by the Church, and Padre Martinez was suspended from the exercise of all priestly functions. He nevertheless continued in his posture as a religious and a revolutionary, and indeed went so far as to set up an independent church. At last Bishop Lamy was obliged to pronounce upon Padre Martinez the most grave sentence of excommunication.

This affair of the schism at Taos polarized sentiment, of course, and there was very nearly an eruption of violence. Those were tense times at Taos.

Willa Cather neglects to mention what are surely the most important accomplishments of this man, the true measures of his genius. Padre Martinez was passionately dedicated to learning, and he spared no effort to further the cause of learning in his parish. To this end he opened a school in which he was himself the principal instructor. Determined that his parishioners, all of them, should be literate, he founded a printing office, the first in New Mexico, in which he printed his own school-books, among other things. And he published a newspaper, *El Crepusculo*, the first in New Mexico. Of his home he made a kind of monastery to which the best young men of his time and place came to study and to formulate ideas.

This is the basis upon which Padre Martinez should be remembered, surely: he made of Taos in the first half of the nineteenth century a center of intellectual activity. Perhaps there is no way to account for such things—or such men. They happen upon us, and they are the pillars of our civilization.

The Octopus

Several years before she died, Georgia O'Keeffe and I were talking about various places we had been, Ghost Ranch among them, where she spent her summer in New Mexico.

"It is simply the place that I like best in the world," she said.

It was not an unlikely statement, but I have been unable to put it out of my mind.

There are places where you feel you have truly invested your life, where you have been alive more intensely than elsewhere. And certain people, too, have a more highly developed sense of place than have others, I believe. They seem to have a better idea of where they are or ought to be. For me this sense of place is a thing of moments.

Once, I wrote in my journal:

> At five o'clock this afternoon I looked out across Monument Valley. The air was very thin and cold. The great rocks were pink and purple and deeply etched with vertical shadows. The floor of the valley reached away to the horizon of darker pink and purple stripes. The valley is stranger and more vast than other places I have known, or it is of another order of strangeness and vastness. As I contemplated the monuments, something powerful happened—a feeling of awful peace and quiet came over me. For a long time, then, it was as if I had happened into the nearest corner of eternity.

On another occasion I went with a friend into Canyon de Chelly, and we slept under a cliff that seemed to ascend to the stars. We dined on steak au poivre and a bottle of Romanée-St.-Vivant. And at sunrise, having eaten cold, crisp apples and drunk coffee laced with brandy, we climbed up to a window in the rock. Far below, like ants, were Navajo men on horseback. They sang their riding songs. Their voices drifted up to us like the scent of sage.

And several years ago, in the early morning, I walked along the beach at Santa Barbara. The tide was out, and there were pools in the sand. Then I saw something in one of the pools, under a large piece of driftwood. It was an octopus, small and motionless, only partly submerged, and it seemed to be dead. It filled me with curiosity, for I had never seen such an unlikely creature before. I stood over it and studied it for a long time, and it did not move. It was supple and stark in the water, the color of bone, and I was afraid to touch it. After a while I got a stick and probed at it. Suddenly it blushed pink and blue and violet, and it began to writhe about. The stiff reaction, total and grotesque, alarmed me, for everything about it seemed to describe some profound agony. It took hold of the stick and clung to it; I carried it away to the surf and laid it down. I supposed that it would go off at once into the depths, but no, it settled again and lay still.

I like to think that it might have been dealing with me, that in its alien, ocean mind, it was struggling to take my presence into account, that I had touched its deep, essential life, and it would never lose the impression that I had made upon it. It was still there when I came away, and it had not moved, except that it rocked very slightly to and fro in the water. And now I wonder, What does it mean that, after these years, I should speak of the octopus? It may be that I saved its life, but I know very little about the life of an octopus, and I shall not presume to say what salvation is worth to either of us. Only just now, as a strange loneliness, it occurs to me that this creature has, for some years now, been of some small consequence in the life of my mind. And I wonder if, in the dark night of the sea, there, deep within its own sphere of instinct, the octopus dreams of me.

Dreaming In Place

On such an evening as this, it is good to dream. It is raining, and a great, gray cloud lies out across the valley of the Rio Grande. Over the Jemez lightning flickers and flashes, and the thunder is so constant as to be subliminal. I crave an audacious music, yet easy, comfortable, native. Copland comes to mind, and I put on *Billy the Kid*. A frontier town looms up in the mind's eye. There is brawling and gunplay. A woman is cut down in the crossfire, and it remains, alas, for her son, a mere lad of twelve, to avenge her death and to flee. In that awful moment of pain and rage his whole destiny is determined. The music swells upon me, and I am carried along in the swift current of his legend: night on the prairie, a card game, a gunfight, capture and escape, and, at last, death in the desert. The evocation is all but irresistible, and an epic notion of heroism lies at the center of it.

We Americans have always cherished the institution of "the dying cowboy." From the dime novel to the silver screen it has been one of our most perdurable sentiments, an authentic national treasure.

> *We beat the drum slowly and played the fife lowly,*
> *And bitterly wept as we bore him along;*
> *For we all loved our comrade, so brave, young, and handsome,*
> *We all loved our comrade although he'd done wrong.*

But if this is not precisely a false view of Billy the Kid, it is decidedly a partial one. And the irony is that the other side of this particular coin is just as ambiguously true and false; to wit, the famous photograph (the only one known to exist, if I am not mistaken) in which Billy appears to be a mindless, pear-shaped boy—essentially innocuous in spite of the arsenal at his hips—who stands in peculiar relation to man and to God.

The truth is not necessarily to be found in either of these directions. Nor is it to be found at all, necessarily. Men like Billy the Kid are finally unknowable, I suspect; they are revealed, if at all, in flashes of insight that bear not at all upon reason, but that illuminate a person in place, and only momentarily.

There are certain people who by the sheer force of their presence seem to determine the reality of a given place. They have such complete dominion within it that it cannot be said to exist, except in relation to them. I have come upon a few of these person-place equations, these entities, in my time. So have we all. Once I met an old man, an Ojibwa medicine man, who gave me a spoonful of bark-and-herb medicine that tasted rather like sawdust saturated with lemon oil and vinegar. This was beside a lake in Minnesota, where at evening a low mist lay upon the wild rice paddies, and you could see the night coming toward you through the trees. I believed conditionally in the old man's medicine, but I believed absolutely in the old man. He was one with the dark, wooded landscape of that place, and, quite simply, it would not have been the same place without him. I am not convinced, in fact, that it would have *been* at all.

And so it also was with Georgia O'Keeffe and her home at Abiquiu. In the latter I believed conditionally; in the former, absolutely. Moreover, my belief is based upon an unimpeachable logic, as far as I could tell. I have seen photographs of Georgia O'Keeffe abroad, and I know her to be wholly recognizable in the context of the world at large. But I have never been to Abiquiu when she was not there, and therefore I do not believe that her home exists in her absence, though I am willing to believe that it exists in mine.

All in all, it is a complicated system of belief, I admit, but I shall insist upon my interpretation of the affair. After all, that is my right; and, after all, there are modes, and modes, of existence. If a tree falls in the desert, and I am not there to see that it falls, it falls nevertheless. So I am told. But the event has to be perceived, I contend, or else it cannot be said to take place in fact. A thing is realized by means of perception, and not otherwise. Existence itself is illusory; we inhabit a dream in the mind of God.

Once when he had returned from a cattle drive in Mexico, Drum Hadley and I were having a drink on the Plaza in Santa Fe, discoursing alternately, as I recall, in trimeter and pentameter. Drum is surely one of the most easygoing of men, deliberate and imperturbable, essentially in possession of himself. As we got up to leave, I noticed that Drum exchanged nods with a man in the doorway, a drifter as far as I could tell, and no doubt an acquaintance of long standing, so much of pure recognition was there in the moment at which their eyes met. On the street I remarked upon this matter, venturing to guess that the two men had traveled and drunk together in other days. "No," Drum replied, "I never saw him before. But he is a *vaquero*, a real one, and there is a look about such men." I pondered this, and in a moment I was nearly overcome with something like loneliness, a sense of exclusion and disaffection. It was a strange moment for me, the moment of truth and exile, as it were. I was an Indian among cowboys.

About the Author

N. Scott Momaday is a poet, novelist, painter, playwright, and story-teller. He resides in the American Southwest, and he is Regents' Pro-fessor of English at the University of Arizona. Among his numerous awards are the Academy of American Poets Prize, the Pulitzer Prize, and the Premio Letterario Internazionale "Mondello," Italy's highest literary award. He is a member of the Kiowa Gourd Dance Society and a Fellow of the American Academy of Arts and Sciences.